MEASURED BY THE SOUL

The Life of Joseph Carey Merrick
ALSO KNOWN AS, THE ELEPHANT MAN

Jeanette Sitton & Mae Siu-Wai Stroshane

A PUBLICATION OF THE FRIENDS OF JOSEPH CAREY MERRICK

'Tis true my form is something odd
But blaming me is blaming God
Could I create myself anew
I would not fail in pleasing you.

If I could reach from pole to pole
Or grasp the ocean with a span
I would be measured by the soul
The mind's the standard of the man.'

a poem Joseph Merrick often quoted, to end his letters.
- adapted from "False Greatness" by Isaac Watts.

COVER PHOTOGRAPH: Brooke Scovil (FoJCM)
Copyright 2012. All rights reserved.

FRIENDS OF JOSEPH CAREY MERRICK LOGO: Audrey Kantrowitz (FoJCM)
Copyright 2012. All rights reserved.

© 2012 Jeanette Sitton & Mae Siu-Wai Stroshane. All rights reserved.
ISBN 978-1-300-45725-1

DEDICATION

This book is dedicated to our friends who live with Proteus Syndrome: Jordan Whitewood-Neal, Lisa Bartlett, and Brian Richards. They have generously shared their experiences, so as to educate us and enrich our understanding of how they cope with this extremely rare and devastating disorder. Thanks to the dedication of Dr. Leslie Biesecker and his team of geneticists at the National Institute of Health Human Genome Project, people with Proteus have new hopes for its treatment and ultimate cure.

ACKNOWLEDGEMENTS

We have many friends to thank for helping us write this book. Any omissions are entirely ours. Many thanks to the Friends of Joseph Carey Merrick (FoJCM) for their dedication and devotion to keeping Joseph's legacy alive through the years; Stephen Butt, Leicester historian and Friend of Joseph Carey Merrick, who has donated his time, expert advice, and practical help in researching Joseph's life in Leicester; Jonathan Evans, Archivist and Curator at the Royal London Hospital Museum, who has shared his extensive knowledge of Joseph's history, as well as access to Joseph's surviving memorabilia; Emma-Jane Hartley, who travelled to Fawsley Estate and walked in Joseph's footsteps; Peter Cousins, of the Rutland County Registrar's Office who confirmed the location of Mary Jane (Potterton) Merrick's grave; The Friends of Welford Road Cemetery, who sifted through registers and microfiche to locate the grave of Mary Jane's children; the Record Office for Leicestershire, Leicester and Rutland; Lynda Smart, of the Leicester Mercury newspaper; Moat Community College, who have given Joseph's memorial plaque a permanent home; the British Library; Rob Dale, for permission to use his wealth of information on the Merrick family tree; Reverend Thomas Clay for his unique and insightful essay on the painstaking construction of a modern-day prototype of Joseph's cardboard cathedral; Maya Stroshane, for early proofreading of the manuscript and finally, a special thank you to Jeffrey Timmons (FoJCM), for his careful editing of the manuscript, and insightful comments during the creation of this book.

ABOUT THE AUTHORS

Jeanette Sitton a London, UK resident is a wildlife photographer and is co-Founder of Lee Valley Bats, a voluntary, community group, dedicated to helping bats through mitigation, education and community action.

In 1990, Jeanette founded the Joseph Carey Merrick Tribute website. It began with just a few sample articles about this man's courageous life. There are now over 50 pages.

In 1995, she went on to found the Friends of Joseph Carey Merrick, devoted to keeping Joseph's inspiring story alive. The group raises funds for Proteus Syndrome research and to assist and benefit Proteus Syndrome patients.

--

Mae Siu-Wai Stroshane lives in Boston, Massachusetts, USA. She has published short stories in numerous anthologies, including *The Forbidden Stitch: Stories of Asian American Women,* winner of the National Book Award, (Calyx Press, 1990), "Prentice-Hall Gold Series of Literature," and *A Ghost At Heart's Edge: Stories and Poems of Adoption* (North Atlantic Press, 2002). Her story about Joseph's last Easter, *A Stranger in the Garden,* has appeared in numerous literary magazines. She is a researcher for the Friends of Joseph Carey Merrick.

TABLE OF CONTENTS

Dedication
Acknowledgements
About the authors
Introduction

MEASURED BY THE SOUL

Chapter One: The Real *Elephant Man*	8
Chapter Two: Childhood Lost	12
Chapter Three: The Workhouse	22
Chapter Four: *The Elephant Man*	27
Chapter Five: The Showman and the Surgeon	45
Chapter Six: Winter's Chill	50
Chapter Seven: A Home at Last	55
Chapter Eight: Angels of Mercy	68
Chapter Nine: A Christmas to Remember	81
Chapter Ten: Fresh Air and Freedom	86
Chapter Eleven: Peace at Last	90

EPILOGUE

A commemorative plaque for Joseph Merrick	95
Significant dates	97

SUPPLEMENTAL ARTICLES

- The Autobiography of Joseph Carey Merrick	104
- *The Elephant Man,* a medical article by Frederick Treves, New York Medication Abstract British Medical Journal, Dec 11th, 1886	107
- Sir Frederick Treves: a biography	109
- Carr-Gomm's second letter to the Times, January 1887	111

INTRODUCTION
by Jeanette Sitton,
Founder, Friends of Joseph Carey Merrick

I began the 'Joseph Carey Merrick Tribute' website in 1993. It started out with just one or two pages of researched material, but it soon became a hit. There are now over fifty pages at www.josephcareymerrick.com

A dear friend of mine, George, (now passed away), had ankylosing spondylitis and ulcerative colitis. His spine was disfigured and, having fused cervical vertebrae, he was unable to move his head. To look upwards, he would precariously tilt back on his heals and he regularly fell.

Like so many people with disabilities, George was determined to lead a full life. He painted several large oil paintings, taller than he was.

Like Joseph, he had also experienced painful ordeals: the hurtful remarks, the staring, the pointing and laughter. But he would shrug it off. I saw so much of Joseph's character in my friend. He was gentle, quietly spoken, kind and, although he had more than his fair share of reasons to be angry - I never heard him say a bad word about anyone. George was my inspiration for the tribute website and for co-authoring this fundraising book.

Royal London Hospital, Whitechapel
(The Mirror)

Chapter 1

THE REAL *ELEPHANT MAN*

Who was *The Elephant Man*, and why does his story continue to haunt us, more than one hundred and twenty years after his death? In addition to the film, his life has been celebrated in plays, fiction, and at least one book of poetry.[1] If one types the name "Joseph Merrick" into the Google search bar on the Internet, hundreds of articles, photographs, images, and videos surface. Some are scientific articles or tender tributes to his memory. Sadly, others are mocking parodies of his impaired manner of walking and talking. The words *"Elephant Man"* are casually bandied about as cruel shorthand for something ugly, strange, and different. The association with elephants calls to mind something wild, dangerous and beastly. This is a disservice not only to elephants, which are remarkably intelligent, loyal and affectionate,[2] but most of all, to Joseph Merrick, a man whose never-ending quest for human dignity touched the hearts of those who came to know him.[3]

Joseph Carey Merrick suffered from a disfiguring condition that baffled medical experts and often terrified those who encountered him in person.[4] Unable to work in the everyday world, he embarked on a short career on the fairground circuit, taking on an indelible show name that captured the imagination of the audience and brought him lasting fame. In an era that often thought in stark terms of good vs. evil, a name like *"The Elephant Man"* conjured up images of something wild and dangerous, a monstrous being even capable of murder.[5]

However, those who knew Joseph Merrick, especially Frederick Treves, the London Hospital surgeon who sheltered and befriended him in his last years, were struck by his gentleness and forgiving nature towards his persecutors.[6] His strong moral character and quiet courage in the face of overwhelming adversity earned their respect and admiration. More than one person remarked on his strong religious faith.[7] This was no accident. Joseph's mother, Mary Jane Merrick, was a devout Sunday School teacher who nurtured her son through times of painful illness and taught him the Bible. [8] Paradoxically, this enlightened, educated woman harboured an ancient superstition that gave rise to the *"Elephant Man"* legend, which took on mythical proportions even during his lifetime. It has endured to this day.

Our story begins on a chilly day in December, 1861, when Mary Jane Potterton married a young cab driver named Joseph Rockley Merrick. Mary Jane had turned twenty-six the previous month and was already four weeks pregnant. Rockley, age twenty-four, was living with his widowed mother, Sarah, and younger brother, Charles, at the time.[9]

The wedding took place at St. Michael's and All Angels Church, a lovely stone edifice in Thurmaston, a borough four miles from the centre of Leicester. Perhaps the occasion was a poignant mix of joy and sorrow, for Mary Jane's mother, Elizabeth, had died earlier that year at the age of 54. [10] Though the newly-wedded couple began married life in the Merrick family home, they soon moved out and established their own household a few doors down at 50 Lee Street. Perhaps Sarah came to help when Mary Jane's child was born on 5 August, 1862. He was christened "Joseph" after his father, and for a middle name, his mother chose the name "Carey" in honour of the famous Baptist minister, William Carey, who ministered to the poor in Leicester.[11]

Life was precarious for infants in Victorian times, but little Joseph seems to have thrived in his early months. According to an anonymous article that appeared in the Leicester Chronicle, on December 29th, 1930, [12] Joseph was a *"perfect baby"* at birth, with no sign of the physical changes to come. But a flaw in his appearance began to emerge when he was about twenty months.

9

Mary Jane first noticed a small swelling under her son's upper lip on the right side. The growth grew larger and firmer, eventually pushing his upper lip outward. In her mind, the writer states, this tumour began to resemble an elephant's trunk.

In later years, Mary Jane told Joseph that his condition was a result of her being badly frightened by an elephant in the sixth month of her pregnancy. She had gone to see Wombwell's Circus in nearby Humberstone Gate, a wide thoroughfare that regularly hosted travelling fairs and sideshows. Every day at noon, the circus paraded its elephants through the streets, as a walking advertisement. In the press of the excited crowd, Mary Jane was knocked down in the path of a passing elephant, scrambling to her feet just in time to avoid injury.[13]

Like many other mothers of her time, she believed in 'maternal impression,' the notion that misfortunes during pregnancy could leave their mark on the unborn child. All his life, Joseph took comfort in this story, believing that this explained his deformities. In his sideshow pamphlet, *The Autobiography of Joseph Carey Merrick,* he wrote:

"The deformity which I am now exhibiting was caused by my mother being frightened by an Elephant; my mother was going along the street when a procession of Animals were passing by, there was a terrible crush of people to see them, and unfortunately she was pushed under the Elephant's feet, which frightened her very much; this occurring during a time of pregnancy was the cause of my deformity."[14]

The hard swelling in Joseph's mouth continued to grow, and bumps appeared on the left side of his torso. Mary Jane, pregnant again, no doubt worried whether the new baby would be healthy. She gave birth to her second son on 21 April, 1864, and christened him John Thomas.[15] The existence of little John Thomas has only recently been discovered, bringing the total number of Mary Jane and Rockley's children to four. The records do not show whether the new baby was healthy at birth, but his death certificate states that he died of variola, or smallpox, at only three months of age. His name appears in the burial records of Welford Road Cemetery in July of 1864, just weeks before Joseph's second birthday. [16]

Sadly, John Thomas's death was all too common in those days when parents could expect to bury at least one child. Perhaps Rockley felt cheated of another healthy son, and his later animosity towards young Joseph dates back to this loss. While this does not exonerate him in any way for his physical abuse of Joseph, it might explain the frustration he felt, seeing his hopes for a prosperous family dashed time after time. His and Mary Jane's early joy was to be short-lived.

Footnotes:
[1] Graham, Peter & Oeschlaeger, Fritz, *Articulating the Elephant Man: Joseph Merrick and His Interpreters,* The Johns Hopkins University Press, pp 1 – 2
[2] Sheldrick, Daphne, DBE, *Love, Life, and Elephants: An African Love Story,* Viking Press, 2012
[3] Graham, Peter & Oeschlaeger, Fritz, *Articulating the Elephant Man: Joseph Merrick and His Interpreters,* The Johns Hopkins University Press, p. 4
[4] ibid, p. 2
[5] ibid, p. 2
[6] ibid, p. 6
[7] Howell & Ford, "The True History of the Elephant Man," p. 80
[8] bid, p. 188
[9] http://members.iinet.net.au/~kjstew/MERIK3.htm
[10] Ibid.
[11] Howell & Ford, "The True History of the Elephant Man," p. 42
[12] Ibid, p. 42
[13] Ibid, p. 42
[14] bid, p. 173
[15] http://members.iinet.net.au/~kjstew/MERIK3.htm
[16] ibid.

Chapter 2

CHILDHOOD LOST

Despite their life of poverty, Mary Jane bequeathed gifts to her son that would serve him well all his life: a love of books and a deep Christian faith. No doubt many times Joseph was forced to seek comfort in both, especially after he suffered a severe fall when he was five. His left hip became infected and left him barely able to walk without a cane.

To give Joseph as normal a life as possible, she sent him to school with the other children. He attended Syston Street School until the age of twelve and is believed to have attended Archdeacon Lane Baptist Church, where Mary Jane taught Sunday school.[1]

By now, Joseph's deformities undoubtedly drew unwanted attention from his schoolmates. Bony lumps were growing on his forehead, his spine began to twist in a corkscrew turn, and he walked with a limp. If he had to endure any teasing or bullying by his classmates, he wouldn't have been able to get away from them.

In 1865, Rockley took a new job as a stoker on a steam engine in one of Leicester's cotton factories.[2] He moved the family from Lee Street to 119 Upper Brunswick Street, where they remained for the next three years. During that time, Mary Jane gave birth to two more children, William Arthur and Marion Eliza. Her growing family kept her busy, and Joseph's increasing disabilities must have been worrisome.

Restless and ambitious, Rockley received a promotion to 'engine driver' at the factory. He also yearned to become his own boss; his name appeared in the Leicester Trade Directory as the proprietor of a haberdashery shop at 37 Russell Square.

Unfortunately, the management of the job fell largely to Mary Jane, while her husband continued to work in the factory. Perhaps Joseph was helpful in small ways—sorting gloves and placing the accessories on display, or minding the children during shop hours.

Tragedy hovered over the Merrick family like a lingering fog. Worn down by the cares of raising three children and full-time management of a haberdashery, Mary Jane seemed to lose her strength after William's death. Her own health began to fail, and on 19 May, 1873, she died of bronchial pneumonia.[3]

As a side note, Mary Jane did not die on her birthday, as is often stated. Her birthday was the 20th of November, 1836.[4] Thus, she was thirty-six years and six months of age at her death. She was buried in Welford Road Cemetery in Leicester, where John Thomas and William Arthur had also been laid to rest.[5] Joseph was not quite eleven years old at the time, and losing his mother was one of the greatest sorrows of his life.

After his mother died, Joseph's life took a turn for the worse. Rockley considered him old enough to earn wages and pulled him out of school to look for work. This would prove to be difficult, not only because jobs were few, but also because his *"appearance and crippled state went against him."*[6] Rockley, a widower with two disabled children to provide for, moved the family to 4 Wanlip Street, a rooming house run by a widow named Emma Wood Antill. Emma had two daughters from her previous marriage, Annie and Florence. He paid Emma to cook, clean and look after his children. Less than eighteen months later, however, he married her at the Archdeacon Baptist Lane Church. Eventually, they had three daughters: Cassandra (born 1879), Dora (born 1881) and Pauline (born 1883).[7]

In his sideshow pamphlet, Joseph wrote:

> *"Unfortunately, he* [his father] *married his landlady. Henceforth I never had one moment's comfort, she, having children of her own, and I not being so handsome as they, together with my deformity, she was the means of making my life a perfect misery."*[8]

He recalled that she served him smaller portions than the others at mealtimes or gave him at most greasy scraps. She harangued him about seeking employment and punished him by withholding supper if he came home without success.

After a long search, Joseph found a job at Messrs. Freeman's Cigar Factory, learning to roll tobacco leaves into cigars. He worked there for two years, but when his right hand began to grow clumsy and cumbersome, he was no longer capable of the delicate and precise touch needed for the job.[9] His employer had to let him go and Joseph was back out on the streets again.

Rockley grew impatient with Joseph's inability to find work. He conceived the idea of equipping him with accessories from the haberdashery and sending him out to hawk in the streets of Leicester. Not only that, he insisted that Joseph meet a quota of sales every day. If not, he was often beaten or deprived of his supper.[10]

As Joseph went from house to house with his tray of bootblack, shoelaces, and gloves, a crowd of ridiculing children followed him. His appearance was growing steadily more bizarre, and the mass of flesh growing in his mouth rendered his speech nearly unintelligible. His painful hip left him unable to escape the torment.

Meanwhile, Rockley had moved the family into a house attached to the haberdashery at 37 Russell Square. Painfully, Joseph made his way through the neighbourhood and sometimes stopped off at Leicester's famed Clock Tower in Haymarket Square. A citizen of

Leicester named Mrs. Riley told her grandson years later what she remembered of Joseph's attempts to hawk his wares.

"Freak-Show Attraction Tormented In Our City"
Leicester Mercury Newspaper, 4th September, 2003

"Mr. Riley has written to tell me about his grandmother, who met Merrick when she was a teenager living with her parents in the West End of Leicester. Mr. Riley recalls her telling him that Merrick worked as a door-to-door salesman who sold goods from his parents' shop, in Russell Square, off a tray, which hung round his neck. He also stood at the Clock Tower selling his wares with his name on a card. She remembered the cruelty of people when they saw him. When he came down the street, at least 20 young children would follow him everywhere he went and mocked him, she said."

He was well known in Leicester long before the world knew about him. The life he led here was a horror." As Joseph's appearance worsened, he was driven from his home and his hawker's license was revoked.

As he was unable to earn a living, he was admitted to the Leicester Union Workhouse, where he remained for five years before becoming a 'curiosity' in a freak show." Mr. Riley remembers staying with his grandmother during the war when she was an elderly woman. Clearly Joseph Merrick had made quite an impression on her all those years ago and she felt strongly about the way he was treated. He recalls:

"My grandmother first told us children about Joseph during the Second World War, when we went to stay with her "As children then, we didn't have much and we moaned a lot, as children do. One day, when we were having bread and jam for tea, she told us about Joseph and told us how lucky we were to be born normal. I think she would have liked the image of Joseph in the Mercury—of how he might have looked."[11]

The original tumour in Joseph's mouth continued to grow, his head was nearly the circumference of his waist, and warty flaps of skin hung from his chest and back. It became progressively harder for him to meet the daily quota of sales that Rockley had callously set for him. If he fell short, he was thrashed, with the encouragement of his stepmother.

In his autobiography, Joseph tells us that he would stay out the whole day with a hungry stomach rather than face beatings at home. Several times he ran, or in his words, *"walked away from home, being lame."* He concluded that his father had, *"some spark of parental feeling left, so he induced me to return home again."*[12]

One day when Joseph was fifteen, he failed to meet the daily quota. He had been on such short rations from his stepmother that he was ravenous, and spent his small earnings on food.[13] He knew he would be punished when he got home. He received such a beating that he ran away for good. This time Rockley didn't bother to look for him.

Joseph spent two nights in a lodging house, attempting to sell his wares by day. Then his Uncle, Charles Barnabas, found him and took him into his home for the next two years.[14] Joseph continued to hawk goods around the neighbourhood to help his aunt and uncle with his keep. For the first time since his mother had died, Joseph was living among people who offered him their love and understanding.

Footnotes:

[1] Rob Dale http://www.robshistory.co.uk/josephcareymerrick.html
[2] Howell & Ford, *The True history of the Elephant Man. The Autobiography of Joseph Carey Merrick,* p. 173
[3] ibid, p. 45
[4] http://familytreemaker.genealogy.com/users/c/o/u/Peter-Howard-Cousins/WEBSITE-0001/UHP-0012.html
[5] Burial records from the Friends of Welford Cemetery, Leicester
[6] Howell & Ford, *The True History of the Elephant Man, The Autobiography of Joseph Carey Merrick,"* p. 173
[7] Rob Dale http://www.robshistory.co.uk/josephcareymerrick.html
[8] Howell & Ford, *The True History of the Elephant Man, The Autobiography of Joseph Carey Merrick,* p. 173
[9] ibid., p. 49
[10] ibid. p. 173
[11] http://www.accessmylibrary.com/coms2/summary_0286-24311791_ITM
[12] Howell & Ford, *The True History of the Elephant Man, The Autobiography of Joseph Carey Merrick,* p.173
[13] ibid, p. 50
[14] ibid, p. 50

Thurmaston Parish Church, where Mary Jane Potterton and Joseph Rockley Merrick were wed, December 29, 1861. (Jeanette Sitton, FoJCM. Copyright 2012. All rights reserved).

Humberstone Gate in Leicester, where Mary Jane is said to have been knocked down by a circus elephant when pregnant with Joseph in May, 1862. He always believed his condition was caused by her frightening experience. (Both photos: public domain)

Most of the original Lee Street, where Joseph was born on August 5, 1862, has long gone. This is the only section surviving. Although resurfaced at some point, cobblestones peep through. Now renamed as Lower Lee Street. Joseph's home would have been just a few feet from the dip in the pavement, behind the fencing. (top left) (Jeanette Sitton, FoJCM. Copyright 2012. All rights reserved).

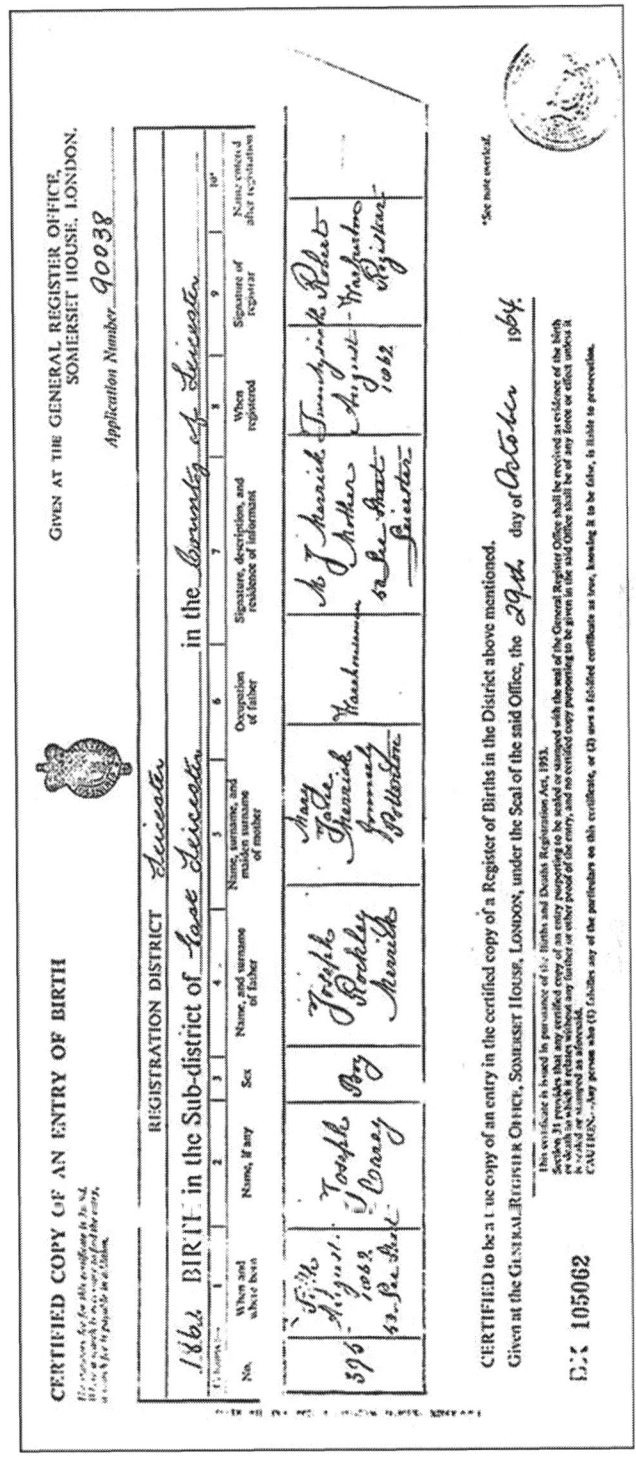

The Birth Certificate of Joseph Carey Merrick. Registered at two years of age.

Chapter 3

THE WORKHOUSE

For two years, Joseph lived with his aunt and uncle and he continued to hawk his wares as best he could. Instead of forcing him to meet a daily quota, Charles accepted whatever he could manage. His Aunt Jane looked after him and helped with his daily care. Joseph's skin growths had begun to emit an unpleasant odour, requiring him to bathe at least daily. Nowadays everyone bathes daily, back then was not the case. Still, he was as comfortable as he ever could be, and it seems Charles took the role of a caring father.

Charles Barnabas was the youngest of the Merrick brothers and left home in his teens to become a barber's apprentice. He learned the trade well. In 1870, he opened his own barbershop at 144 Churchgate and lived upstairs with his wife, Jane. They had their share of tragedies, losing five out of nine children. Their first three children were buried in one plot in the Welford Road Cemetery, and the stark dates of the infants' deaths tell their story:[1]

Arthur Gilbert, died on Aug 31, 1870, aged 2 weeks
Arthur Gilbert died on Dec 12, 1872 aged 14 months
Emma Ada, died on Jul 3, 1877 aged 1 year

The remaining two were buried in the newer Belgrave Cemetery:

George Perry, died on Apr 6, 1886 aged 1 year
Walter Edward, died Aug 26, 1886 aged 9 weeks

Despite their own hard times, Charles and Jane saw their nephew's desperate situation and gave him a home when he needed it most. Later on, Joseph would warmly remember his uncle in *The Autobiography of Joseph Carey Merrick*.[2]

"The best friend I had in those days was my father's brother, Mr. Charles Merrick, Hair Dresser, Church Gate, Leicester."

When Joseph applied to renew his hawking license, the Commissioners For Hackney Carriages turned him down, stating it was *"acting in the public good."*[3] The cranial bulges of bone and tumours were growing increasingly large, invariably drawing in a crowd wherever he went. Devastated, Joseph attempted to find work but no one would hire him, either for his appearance or his disabilities. He walked with a pronounced limp, his head was overgrown and the pink stump in his mouth rendered his speech almost unintelligible. His right arm had become so overgrown, it was unwieldy and of no use.

There were increasing pressures at home as well. Charles' first surviving son, Alfred, was now four years old. Jane became pregnant again in 1879 and later that year gave birth to a healthy daughter, whom she named Alice. Sensitive about being an extra mouth to feed, Joseph saw that he had only one option left.[4]

Much to his regret, Charles had to relinquish his nephew to the Leicester Union Workhouse, a vast Victorian building that stood on Sparkenhoe Street[5] at the site of the present day Moat Community College. However, Joseph understood that his uncle's growing family needed to be provided for first. He stayed on with Charles, Jane and Grandmother Sarah through Christmas. Then, on December 29th, he presented himself at the workhouse gates to plead his case.[6]

William Cartwright, the receiving officer, authorised Joseph's admission. He gave him a pass and sent him up to the admissions block. Joseph's entry in the workhouse records shows that he listed his religion simply as, *"church,"* his occupation as, *"hawker,"* and his reason for needing charity as *"unable to work."* Interestingly, he listed his birth year as 1861. This wasn't the only time he got the date wrong.[7]

After a so-called *"hot bath"*—which in fact, was freezing cold,[8] Joseph was assigned to a group of men ages 16-60. Among them were those classified as *"imbeciles"* and *"idiots,"* to use the language of the day. There were also drunkards, criminals, and other disabled persons. Few were able-bodied. Workhouse conditions were intentionally harsh to discourage shirkers — in other words, to prevent those that were capable of working from living on the dole.[9]

Among the many gruelling jobs that Joseph undertook was oakum picking, which involved beating and pulling apart old rope and rags with a wooden mallet and fingertips. These would be reused to plug ships' hulls to make them watertight. Oakum picking was dirty, difficult, tedious and painful work, made more so by Joseph's inability to use his right hand.

Workhouse life was ruled by the constant clanging of bells to signal rising, eating, stopping and starting work, and going to bed for a few scant hours before starting the routine all over again. The food was plain and far from plentiful—a typical meal was tea and bread, or bread and dripping, but plum pudding was served at Christmas. The inmates were segregated by gender, meaning families were split up during their stay.

After enduring workhouse life for twelve weeks, Joseph signed himself out and tried to find employment again. His appearance and limitations made it all but impossible. He had no choice but to return to the workhouse. This time he would stay there for four long years.[10]

When Joseph signed himself back into the workhouse on that bleak day in March, there were 928 inmates, all classified as paupers.[11] This broad term covered the most infirm denizens of society—the ill, the elderly, unmarried mothers, disabled workers, illegitimate babies and even those classified as *"retarded"* or *"insane."* Although they were all provided with a meal and a bed, the workhouse was never meant to be a comfortable shelter. Those who stayed there permanently usually did so out of desperation or terminal illness, the way Joseph's grandfather had died.[12]

The hours were gruelling for both men and women, who had to meet quotas for wood chopping, corn grinding and granite crushing.[13] Women had to do the laundering for more than six hours daily, hemming and repairing inmate clothes and linen. They also had to prepare and serve the meals in the vast dining halls. Older girls were assigned to watch over younger children, but no special care was arranged for the babies, who lay in filthy cots and never had the chance to breathe fresh air.[14]

The Leicester workhouse was immense, an endless warren of draughty corridors and winding stairs that would have been painful for Joseph to handle. One can imagine him struggling to arrive on time to meals and work, and perhaps he was even the target of kicks and blows, a time he would speak of *"with loathing and horror."*[15]

After approximately two years in the workhouse, Joseph was seen by surgeons at the Leicester Union Infirmary (now the Royal Infirmary).[16] The growth on his upper jaw had continued to grow and was now eight inches long. He could barely close his mouth to keep food from falling out, and grew dangerously malnourished. The doctors urged him to have the growth removed. Despite the high risk of post-operative infection in those days, Joseph consented. The anaesthetic most often used at the time was chloroform.[17]

Joseph was unconscious for the procedure, but, given the primitive state of anaesthetics, he was probably in considerable pain afterwards. At least the growth was mostly gone, and he was able to eat again. His speech was still restricted, but less so.

Meanwhile, he began to see the glimmer of an escape from the workhouse. Allow Joseph to tell us in his own words, how he set the course for his future:

> *"So, thought I, I'll make my living being exhibited about the country. Knowing Mr. Sam Torr, Gladstone Vaults, (or Gaiety Theatre and later, the Hippodrome Theatre), Wharf Street, Leicester, went in for Novelties, I wrote to him, he came to see me, and soon arranged matters..."*[18]

Now, at twenty-one, Joseph had grown into a young man of strong character who had survived nightmarish conditions, yet maintained deep religious convictions. When he signed out of the workhouse and joined Sam Torr's group of human novelties on August 29th, 1884, he must have prayed that he could finally pay his own way in the world with dignity and on his own terms.

Footnotes:

[1] http://www.rootschat.com/forum/index.php?action=printpage;topic=474512.0
[2] Howell, Michael & Peter Ford, *The True History of the Elephant Man, The Autobiography of Joseph Carey Merrick*, p. 174
[3] Howell & Ford, *The True History of the Elephant Man*, p. 51
[4] http://www.genuki.org.uk/big/eng/LEI/Leicester.html
[5] Howell & Ford, *The True History of the Elephant Man*, p. 52
[6] ibid p. 52
[7] ibid p. 53
[8] ibid p. 53
[9] ibid p. 54
[10] ibid p. 57
[11] ibid p. 54
[12] ibid p. 51
[13] ibid p. 56
[14] ibid p. 57
[15] ibid p. 57
[16] ibid p. 58
[17] ibid p. 60
[18] ibid, *The Autobiography of Joseph Carey Merrick*, p. 174

Chapter 4

THE ELEPHANT MAN

And so Joseph Carey Merrick became *The Elephant Man*, the name by which he would be known for the rest of his life and beyond. It's possible that he himself suggested the name, thinking back to his mother's frightening encounter with a circus elephant, which he believed to be the cause of his deformity.

His managers billed him as *The Great Freak of Nature*, *Half-a-Man, Half-an-Elephant*, or simply, *The Elephant Man*. Like other circus nicknames, it was catchy and similar to those of other supposed animal-human hybrids — *The Alligator Man* and *The Monkey Girl*. Years later, a doctor from the London Hospital dryly remarked that Joseph's face reminded him more of a tapir, but supposed that *Tapir Man* wouldn't capture the public's imagination in quite the same way.[1]

As soon as Joseph signed himself out of the workhouse, he reported to the offices of Sam Torr, who took him under his wing for the next few months. When the metal workhouse gates clanged shut behind him for the last time, Joseph probably hoped that life as a travelling novelty would bring him good fortune at last.

Sam Torr had just opened the Gaiety Palace of Varieties on the corner of Wharf Street and Gladstone Street, across the road from Lee Street. Torr planned to stage both popular and high-class entertainment, ranging from comedians and vaudeville acts to orchestral concerts held in a lavish music hall. He had made a name for himself by performing a novelty act called *On the Back of Daddy-O*, wearing a dummy costume that created the illusion of a man carrying him on piggyback around the stage.[2] The Gladstone Vaults were in the basement of the Gaiety Palace: variety acts upstairs and curiosity acts below stairs.[3]

27

Churchgate Street, where Joseph's Uncle Charles ran a barbershop, though not shown here.
(Leicester Mercury)

Archdeacon Lane Baptist Church, where Mary Jane taught Sunday School and Joseph attended church. Joseph's father and stepmother were married here.
(Leicester Mercury)

Boys in Syston Street School, circa 1910. Joseph attended there in the 1860s.
(Leicester Mercury)

The newly discovered grave of Mary Jane Potterton and William Arthur Merrick. Also interred there are her siblings, John, Ann and Elizabeth Potterton. Jeanette Sitton (FoJCM), is shown here, to demonstrate its size of roughly 5ft 2".
(Stephen Butt, FoJCM. Copyright 2012. All rights reserved).

'Fancy work; overalls; blouses; corsets; gloves; hosiery; laces; ribbons; haberdashery; flannels; flannelettes; calicoes; underclothing; maids' dresses; caps and aprons'.

Typical wares of a haberdashery shop.
(Mike Quinn. Copyright 2009. Creative Commons License).

The Clock Tower in Haymarket Square where Joseph often hawked wares from his father's haberdashery.
(Leicester Mercury)

A typical 19th century square in Leicester's poorer quarter.
(Leicester Mercury)

The very definition of novelty meant that every act and performer had to attract audiences with something new and surprising.

Sooner or later, the viewers would clamour for a new act to shock or entertain them. In Joseph's case, the shock of his appearance would wear off after only a few viewings, and he would need to move on to another venue fairly quickly.[4]

Torr solved the problem by forming a consortium of managers in other towns and sideshows who would handle Joseph's travels. These included Mr. J. Ellis of Nottingham, another music hall proprietor; *Professor* Sam Roper, who toured the Midlands with Sam Roper's Fair; George Hitchcock, a traveling showman and manager of *"novelties,"* as they preferred to be called, rather than *"freaks"*[5]; and Tom Norman, a young showman who was just building up several exhibition shops in London.

These showmen knew their trade inside and out. They had worked with fairground acts and knew how to present them in the most captivating way. They coached Joseph in how to best present himself to the curious onlookers, and prepared a show pamphlet for him, *The Autobiography of Joseph Carey Merrick.*[6]

In simple, spare prose, Joseph revealed a sad tale—the death of his mother, which led to his father's remarrying a stepmother who taunted Joseph and deprived him of daily nourishment, forcing him to seek work long after it was clear no one would hire him. Rockley then sent his son out hawking goods from the haberdashery, only to beat him if he failed to meet a daily quota. Conditions grew so painful that Joseph ran – or in his words, *"walked, being lame,"* away from home several times. His father sought him out, until one night when Joseph spent his scant earnings on food and came home empty-handed. Rockley beat Joseph so badly, the young boy left home for good and spent two days at a boarding house, hawking merchandise on his own. As we know, his uncle Charles found him and sheltered him for the next two years.

Joseph closes his autobiography with a heartfelt statement:

"In making my first appearance before the public, who have treated me well, in fact I may say, I am as comfortable now as I was uncomfortable before."

But the most memorable lines in the pamphlet aren't his. In his correspondence, Joseph often quoted the poem that opens this book, adapted from *False Greatness* by Isaac Watts, a composer of hymns. The words must have seemed to him the perfect expression of his sense of self-worth and dignity.[7]

Far from treating him as a wild circus beast, as depicted in the 1980 film, *The Elephant Man*, and the Broadway play of the same name, Joseph's managers treated him with respect, even kindness.[8] They paid all his expenses and split their earnings with him fifty-fifty. He was also allowed to keep all of the profits from sales of the pamphlet, based on Tom Norman's memoirs.

In those first months, Joseph's show was wildly successful. Crowds who were initially revolted by his appearance came to see him in a more sympathetic light upon hearing his story. Joseph's first show, or one of the first, was at the Gaiety Palace in his old neighbourhood in Leicester. Any jeers or mocking from the local audience must have felt inconsequential in the face of the generous earnings he amassed. By the time he went to Belgium some two years later, he had saved over fifty pounds, or close to five thousand pounds in today's rates.[9]

In the last week of November, 1884, Joseph's managers sent him down to London to make his debut in the exhibition shops there. George Hitchcock, nicknamed *Little George*, escorted Joseph on the train to meet Tom Norman, his new manager.

When traveling in public, Joseph disguised himself in a long black coat, woollen muffler, and black hat. The famous *Elephant Man* hat and mask would come later in his career.[10]

Tom Norman had built up a small empire of exhibit shops around London, recruiting novelty acts from all over England. Among those was *Madame Electra*, the Electric Lady who would emit a shock when customers shook her hand; a Professor with a *Man Fish*, and numerous little people. Norman had learned his trade at an early age, and years later in his memoirs, *The Penny Showman* he summed up the spirit of these shows that were a mix of stage patter, tall tales, and some reality. (For the full text of these memoirs, see Appendix G.)

"It was not the show, it was the tale you told."[11] Norman boasted that he could exhibit anything from fleas to *Zulu warriors*, (sailors whom he employed to stand around and make up foreign-sounding words). In one show, Tom claimed to be a friend of the great P.T. Barnum, the founder of the circus dynasty in America. As luck would have it, Barnum himself was in the audience and laughed at Norman's extravagant claim. After the show, Barnum noticed the flashy silver chains and coins that Tom always wore across his waistcoat, and dubbed him the *Silver King*. Tom proudly wore that title for the rest of his life.[12]

Norman was accustomed to tall men, bearded women, little people and conjoined twins, but nothing prepared him for the sight of Joseph Merrick. *"I remember thinking, 'Oh God, I can't use you.' But on looking into this unfortunate man's eyes I could see so much pleading and suffering that a great feeling of pity and sympathy overcame any other emotions I may have had."*[13]

Tom shook Joseph's hand and welcomed him with, *"I'll call you 'Joseph' if I may."* Joseph seemed pleased with the more formal name. When George Hitchcock departed, Tom noticed there was a "spirit of friendship between them" that, *"disposed of the lie contained in the letter in the [London] Times....stating that The Elephant Man was dragged about from town to town...and lived a life that was little better than dismal slavery."* As Norman pointed out, *"Had I attempted to be harsh with him in front of the* audience, I would very soon have had the show recked (sic) and me with it."[14]

Tom had a twelve-year-old helper named Jimmy who served as errand boy and junior show manager. He directed Jimmy to set up a bed for Joseph in the basement of their Whitechapel shop, complete with a curtain for privacy. Joseph seemed pleased with the arrangements, telling Tom *"I don't ever want to go back to that place [the workhouse] again."*[15]

As he prepared to open Joseph's exhibit, Tom was concerned about the garish *Elephant Man* posters that Joseph had brought with him. They depicted a sort of half-man half-monster, *"rampaging through a jungle,"* whereas the small, soft-spoken Merrick*", was not capable of much more than a somewhat erratic walk."*[16] So Tom devised a bit of show patter to explain that the Elephant Man was there not to, *"frighten you but to enlighten you."*[17] However, he also made sure to advise ladies, *"in a delicate state of health",* to leave while the curtain was still closed.

Tom's introduction to Joseph included the story of his mother being knocked down by a wild elephant:

> *"Ladies and gentleman...I would like to introduce Mr. Joseph Merrick, the Elephant Man...Brace yourself up to witness one who is probably the most remarkable human ever to draw the breath of life."*[18]

Even though he presented Joseph as odd and different, he emphasised the young man's common humanity with his audience:

> *"Remember, we do not make ourselves, and were you to prick or cut Joseph, he would bleed and that bleed or blood would be red, the same as yours or mine."*[19]

Tom recalled in his memoirs that after the first moments of shock and horror, audiences were mostly sympathetic, and Joseph seemed quite contented with their work together. *"Much more I could write about the bond between Joseph and myself. He was a man of very strong character and beliefs – anxious to earn his own living and be independent of charity".*[20]

The crowds were plentiful, and all of Joseph's penny pamphlets sold out. Tom promptly ordered new ones. Before they arrived, a fellow showman suggested they *"work the nobbings,"* a showman's term for passing the hat, but Joseph found this an affront to his dignity. He turned to Tom at once and said, *"We are not beggars, are we, Thomas?"*[21]

Tom Norman felt that their collaboration could have continued much longer had it not been for a particular client who showed up one day and asked for a private showing. However, historian Gerry LeFurgy cautions us that when reading Norman's memoirs, we should remember that he was anxious to defend his reputation as a reputable, long-established showman who provided a comfortable living for Joseph, and was not, as Treves claimed, *"little more than a drunken, abusive owner"*.[22]

Unfortunately, Tom and Joseph's separation was closer than they imagined, beginning when medical students and other doctors from the London Hospital crossed the road to see Joseph's show. One of them in particular, the hospital obstetrician, Reginald Tuckett, carried his impressions back to his superior, surgeon, Frederick Treves. *"The fateful day Mr. Treves came to see Joseph for himself, would change all of their lives forever."*

Footnotes:

[1] D.G. Halsted *A Doctor in the Nineties*
[2] Howell & Ford, *The True History of the Elephant Man*, p. 62

[3]	An employer of Hex Holdings, (recent occupiers of the Gaiety Place) invited Jeanette Sitton and Rebecca Timmons to go downstairs to see the Vaults. It was closed up for the day, but they were asked if they would like to go back the next day. Unfortunately there wasn't time.
[4]	Howell & Ford, *The True History of the Elephant Man*, p. 62
[5]	ibid., p. 63
[6]	ibid., p.174, Appendix One: *The Autobiography of Joseph Carey Merrick*
[7]	ibid., p 175
[8]	ibid., p. 80
[9]	ibid., p. 83
[10]	*The Penny Showman* by Tom Norman (privately published 1985, British Library)
[11]	http://nfa.dept.shef.ac.uk/history/shows/norman.html
[12]	*The Penny Showman* by Tom Norman (privately published 1985, British Library)
[13]	ibid.
[14]	ibid.
[15]	ibid.
[16]	ibid
[17]	ibid.
[18]	ibid.
[19]	ibid.
[20]	ibid.
[21]	ibid.
[22]	LeFurgy, Gerry. See Appendix F, Frederick Treves vs. Tom Norman, Another perspective.

The workhouse entry for December 29th, 1879, showing Joseph's first workhouse entry (second line). His occupation is listed as "hawker," the church is left blank, and he gives his birth year as 1861.
(Leicester Mercury)

Leicester Union Workhouse, where Joseph lived and worked from 1879 to 1883
(Leicester Mercury)

Inmates of the Whitechapel Workhouse, a short distance from the London Hospital and Spitalfields.
(Peter Higginbotham. Copyright 2012. All rights reserved).

The family grave of the Merrick family. The resting place of Marion Eliza Merrick, Joseph Rockley Merrick, and Emma Wood-Antill Merrick, Belgrave Cemetery, Leicester.
(Peter Cousins. Copyright 2012. All rights reserved).

Chapter 5

THE SHOWMAN AND THE SURGEON

Across the Whitechapel Road, from Tom Norman's exhibition shop, stood the London Hospital, known today as the Royal London Hospital. In the nineteenth century it served the poorest areas of the city, predominantly the East End, covering such areas as Aldgate, Bethnal Green, Spitalfields and Whitechapel. Patients were treated for everything from injuries, (including gang-related ones), infections, and industrial accidents to illegal abortions and attempts of suicide. In English common law, suicide and attempted suicide were illegal until 1961. They were considered immoral, criminal offences against God.[1]

Norman noticed that groups of medical students were crossing Whitechapel Road to see Joseph's show, no doubt attracted by the garish Elephant Man posters. They often stayed afterwards, to ask questions and see Joseph up close. As word spread among their medical colleagues, more began to visit. Tom didn't mind the extra earnings, but the lingering students interfered with the next scheduled viewing. Finally he had to ask them to, *"clear the shop promptly."*[2]

One day, a young man from the hospital stopped in and asked if he might have a private showing of the Elephant Man. Tom liked his visitor's pleasant manners. He introduced himself as Dr. Reginald Tuckett from the London Hospital, and spoke of a colleague, whom he thought would be very interested in coming over. He wondered if that gentleman might also have a private viewing. Tom and Joseph consented.

Early the next morning, when Tom was ordering breakfast at Jack Winder's, a nearby coffee shop, a tall gentleman showed up and announced himself as Frederick Treves, a surgeon and anatomist at the hospital. Tom was buying some *doorsteps,* [thick slices of bread] and coffee for himself, Joseph and Jimmy. According to Norman, Treves grew somewhat irritated because he had to wait.[3]

When he was finished, Tom Norman unlocked the door of 123 Whitechapel Road and led Treves inside. Norman introduced *The Elephant Man* with his usual story about the mother whose frightening encounter with an elephant had forever marked the child in her womb. Treves, a practical man of medicine, impatiently waved away the showman's patter.[4] Norman was scornful of the doctor's eagerness to gaze upon a man who would be no more than a specimen to him. Already the two men were undoubtedly at odds.

Behind the curtain, Joseph Merrick awaited his cue to face his most distinguished audience. One can only imagine what was passing through his mind.

After months on the road, Joseph was probably accustomed to being stared at by audiences from many walks of life, in many venues—the blaring, raucous fairgrounds and the lavish entertainment halls. Although he was undoubtedly laughed at and mocked by some customers, others seemed sympathetic and even moved by his ordeal.

The medical man studied Joseph from every angle. In the film, Frederick Treves is shown gazing upon Merrick with such horror and pity that a single tear rolls down his cheek. Perhaps the real Treves shed a tear the moment he saw Joseph, but not likely. He was known to be a vigorous man with a biting, sarcastic wit and a rare lack of Victorian sentimentality. Initially, his interest in Merrick was solely driven by the urge to diagnose the man's *"chaotic anatomical wilderness."*[5] Treves asked Tom Norman if he might interview and study Merrick in his office at the London Hospital. Perhaps extra money changed hands, but in any case, Joseph was agreeable to the idea.

In his memoirs, *The Elephant Man and Other Reminiscences*, Treves made much of Merrick's need to wear a disguise in public. He describes an enormous yachting cap adorned with a one-eyed mask that would completely hide Joseph's face, and a black robe that swept the floor. A pair of baggy canvas slippers that covered Joseph's overgrown feet completed the outfit. Actually, this dramatic disguise wasn't made for him until he toured with Sam Roper's Fair later in the winter. This is just one example of Treves's embellishments or inaccuracies in his memoirs.[6]

To transport *The Elephant Man* across the wide road to the London Hospital without causing unwanted attention, Treves suggested he be brought in a cab. He gave Joseph his business card, to show to the attendant in the guardhouse. This card would play a huge and vital role in saving Joseph's life two years later.

In his memoirs, Treves gives the impression that he met and examined *The Elephant Man* once, and that when he returned for a second visit, the show had been closed. Again, this is a misrepresentation of his involvement with Joseph. He examined him, took detailed measurements of his body and took photographs. He arranged to present him, in person, at a meeting of the Pathological Society on December 2, 1884.[7]

Treves' colleagues were startled by Joseph's condition, but none could offer a helpful diagnosis. One early theory was elephantiasis. The term might sound similar to Joseph Merrick's show name, but it is a tropical disease caused by a parasitic hair like worm.[8] Typical symptoms of which are thickening of the skin and underlying tissues, especially in the legs and genitals. Joseph had never been in the tropics, nor were his genitals affected.

In 1886, Treves published his findings in the British Journal of Medicine and referred to Joseph's condition as *"pachy-*

47

*dermatocele, with hypertrophy of the long bones."*⁹ Even in the medical mind, Joseph would forever be linked with elephants.

Meanwhile, Joseph's hopes for a cure must have been crushed, yet Treves examined him on at least two or three more occasions. One day he requested that he be brought over to the hospital and shown to some distinguished colleagues, but Joseph refused. According to Tom Norman, *"Treves could hardly control his rage."* But Joseph would not be budged. He had told Tom that he didn't mind being displayed discreetly for a paying audience, but he'd had enough of being handled like a medical specimen. *"I was stripped naked... and felt like an animal in a cattle market."*¹⁰

Only a few days later, the police came to shut down Tom Norman's show *"on grounds of indecency."* This had been happening more and more among the other showmen as well, but in his memoirs, Tom always suspected there was a connection between the closure of his show and his refusal to let Treves see Joseph one more time, without paying.¹¹

Having to close their lucrative show meant not only a loss of income but also the breakup of a partnership that, in Tom's opinion, had gone well. It meant that Joseph would have to return to touring the Midlands instead of remaining in a stable position in London. He confided in Tom that he had hoped to put his savings towards a house in the countryside. This dream might well have become a reality had they not been forced to part.¹²

Norman always felt that Frederick Treves had slandered him, portraying him as a sullen drunk who spoke to his human exhibit *"harshly, as if to a dog."*¹³ This might well be Treves's bias.

Frederick Treves was a brilliant scientist and gifted writer, who eventually published four travel books as well as award-winning medical texts. Had he not chosen to relate Joseph's story amid the *"army of the queer unknown patients"* he had known, Merrick would have remained a medical oddity in a dusty professional journal of a century ago. However, the contrast of his portrayal of Tom Norman in his memoirs, and Norman's own account is striking. As historian Gerry LeFurgy points out in his article in Appendix G, the truth may lie somewhere between, or it could be off the charts. Over a century later, we can only form our own conclusions based on the known facts.

Footnotes

- [1] http://www.samaritans.org/news/press-release-suicide-still-taboo-50-years-after-decriminalisation
- [2] From Tom Norman's memoirs, *The Penny Showman* privately published by his son George Norman in 1986. (British Library)
- [3] ibid.
- [4] ibid.
- [5] Howell & Ford, *The True History of the Elephant Man* p.23
- [6] Howell & Ford, T*he Elephant Man and Other Reminiscences* by Frederick Treves, p. 184
- [7] ibid p.26
- [8] Birrie H, Balcha F, Jemaneh L. *Elephantiasis in Pawe settlement area: podoconiosis or bancroftian filariasis?* Ethiop Med J 35: 245–250
- [9] Treves, Frederick. British Medical Journal, 1886
- [10] From Tom Norman's memoirs, *The Penny Showman,* page 107
- [11] ibid.
- [12] ibid
- [13] Howell & Ford, *The Elephant Man and Other Reminiscences* by Frederick Treves, p. 182

Chapter 6

WINTER'S CHILL

After his disappointing London venture, Joseph returned to Leicester while his managers decided what to do with him next. This was an unexpected turn of events, as everyone had hoped that Joseph's show would be a hit.

But trouble had been brewing on the freak show circuit for several months now, as public outcry against the exhibition of ill, or deformed, individuals caused police to shut down the shows. Joseph's show had drawn increasingly negative reactions. Audiences were worried that he might be carrying some dread contagious disease,[1] or felt that his situation was too horrifying to qualify as entertainment.

As Tom Norman had observed, an act was most successful when the showman spun a tall tale to delight the audience, and make them feel as if they were in on the joke. Most show-goers happily parted with their pennies to see trained fleas and shake hands with *Madame Electra*, whose touch would literally shock them. (A damp plate rigged to an electrical device under her chair gave her the illusion of being full of electricity.)[2]

Perhaps Joseph was feeling dispirited by the separation from Tom Norman, as well as disappointed, by the lack of answers from the medical experts on his condition. His only compensation for his time among them was a set of medical photographs taken by Treves during their first encounter. One image was copied for the cover of Joseph's show pamphlet, but the artist took the liberty of drawing in the trunk that had been removed from Joseph's upper lip two years before.

In January of 1885, Sam Roper signed Joseph to tour with his fair. He was given his own wagon for privacy.[3] He provided

Joseph with *The Elephant Man* disguise —the enormous hat, flannel mask, and voluminous black cloak that hid his features and kept him warm during those chilly months on the road.

Between shows, local boys harassed Joseph, following him around and trying to peek under his cloak. Fortunately, a short muscular boxer named Harry Bramley came to his rescue by knocking the ringleader out cold. The boxer and his cousin Bertram Dooley, billed as *Roper's midgets*, became Joseph's closest friends and bodyguards.

Bertram Dooley's grandson, William, later recalled his grandfather's stories that described, *The Elephant Man* as *"a most interesting man,"* conversant on topics, *"you wouldn't think a man in his condition would talk about."* Dooley was impressed with Joseph's wide range of interests, and remarked that Merrick was a *"bit on the religious side."*[4] (Only one month before, Frederick Treves had described Joseph's speech as *"unintelligible"* and concluded that Joseph was an *"imbecile from birth."*)[5] Once again, Joseph appeared to be settled in a lucrative job among friends and fellow sideshow performers. But the police continued to shut down the show on grounds of public indecency and fears that he carried a contagious disease. Sam Roper grew worried by the increasing intervention of the police. Finally he felt he had no choice but to let Joseph go.

According to a letter written to the London Times by Francis Carr-Gomm, governor of the London Hospital, it was *"an Austrian"* manager who signed up Joseph on a tour of the Continent.[6] William Dooley, on the other hand, recalls that the manager was an Italian named Ferrari, *"the same as a Cockney Italian, like the ice-cream version."*[7] In any case, this manager confidently lined up an extensive itinerary. Though Joseph's friends were probably sad to see him leave, he must have been eager to travel and see new sights. To a young man who had spent most of his life in city slums and a Poor Law workhouse, the chance to travel abroad would have been an adventure.

His new manager took him across the Channel to Belgium, where the police were rumoured to look the other way in exchange for bribes. After only a few weeks, however, the Belgian police turned out to be less tolerant than expected. Like their English counterparts, they shut down Joseph's show on grounds of public indecency.

One morning Joseph awoke to find that his manager had abandoned him and stolen his savings as well. He was now alone in a foreign country where he couldn't speak the language or make himself fully understood.

Destitute and starving, Joseph pawned his few belongings and made his way to Ostend, where he could take a packet ship, (a vessel employed to carry Post Office mail packets to and from British embassies), home to England. He was dealt another blow when the captain refused to let him on board. A doctor named Wardell Cardew gave him brief shelter and medical care. Afterwards, Cardew wrote to his colleague, William Kendal, whose wife, Madge, would play a critical role in Joseph's life: *"I have had the most awful case in my care at Ostend."*[7]

Cardew advised Joseph to make his way to Antwerp, where he could book passage on a boat train back to Harwich. This time he was allowed to board. It was a difficult journey, one hundred and fifty miles across the North Sea by night.[8]

At this point in Joseph's life, he had absolutely no future prospects, no one to turn to for help. The Leicester workhouse would receive him permanently, but as he had vehemently told Tom Norman, *"I don't ever want to go back to that place."*[9] Nor did it seem that he could seek help from Merrick relatives in Spitalfields. Perhaps he didn't even know of their existence.

Joseph arrived at London's Liverpool Street Station at six o' clock in the morning. A clamouring crowd soon formed around him, tormenting him and trying to pull off his disguise. He might have been badly injured had the London police not intervened and escorted him to a third-class waiting room for protection. Exhausted and starving, Joseph collapsed in a heap in a corner. Having rescued him from the mob, the police didn't know what to do with him next.

They searched Joseph for some form of identification. All he had, inside a pocket, was the business card given him two years earlier by Frederick Treves.

Treves was quickly sent for and arrived, pushing his way through the noisy crowd.[11] After one moment of startled recognition, he took charge of Joseph and drove him back to the London Hospital. He didn't have a clear plan in mind other than to rescue him from further mobbing. If Treves had once been a scientist, (regarding Joseph mainly as an unusual medical specimen), he now acted as a physician pledged to alleviate human suffering. Clearly, on that memorable June day, Joseph Merrick was the very epitome of suffering.

At the hospital, Treves smuggled Joseph into an attic ward, instead of officially admitting him. The need for secrecy was twofold: Joseph's appearance would have undoubtedly caused pandemonium in the general wards, and hospital policy did not accept chronic cases. With close to 75,000 patients passing through the London's doors each year, there was no room for patients whose conditions were considered incurable.

The attic room known as the Isolation Ward was ideally situated for patients with a contagious illness or delirium. Treves settled Joseph there and called upon a nurse who could discreetly look after him. This was Nurse Emma Ireland of Cotton Ward, a probationer, or student, who had just completed her training. She provided Joseph with food, a wash and a comfortable bed. He was allowed to rest for the time being, but the question of his future was far from solved.[12]

Footnotes

[1] Howell & Ford, *The True History of the Elephant Man*, p 81
[2] From Tom Norman's Memoirs, *The Penny Showman* pub. 1985 by his family (The British Family)
[3] Howell & Ford, *The True History of the Elephant Man*, p 80
[4] ibid. interview with William Dooley, p 80
[5] Frederick Treves, *The Elephant Man and Other Reminiscences*
[6] Carr-Gomm, letter to the *London Times*, December, 1885 and William Dooley, unpublished interview
[7] Howell &Ford, *The True History of the Elephant Man*, p. 80
[8] ibid p.86
[9] From Tom Norman's memoirs, *The Penny Showman*
[10] Descendants of Charles Barnes Merrick of Victoria, http://members.iinet.net.au/~kjstew/MERIK3.htm
[11] Frederick Treves, *The Elephant Man and Other Reminiscences*
[12] ibid.

Chapter 7

A HOME AT LAST

On that first morning in the Isolation Ward, Joseph fell into an exhausted sleep, sitting with his head propped up against pillows in its accustomed position.

Suddenly, he was jerked awake by a shrill scream. A maid bringing his breakfast had not been forewarned of his appearance. She dropped the tray and fled, leaving splattered gruel[1] and broken crockery on the floor. Years afterwards, Treves remarked in his memoirs that Joseph seemed *"too weak to notice much, but the experience, I am afraid, was not new to him."*[2]

On the contrary, Joseph was acutely aware of his appearance, and extremely sensitive to others' reactions to him.[3] During those early months, Treves observed that Merrick's *"sole idea of happiness was to creep into the darkness and hide."*[4] He disliked being handled and bathed by the nurses,[5] and trembled with fear when unexpected visitors opened his door.[6]

While Treves tried to find a permanent home for Joseph, the young man expressed a fervent wish to live in a lighthouse or a home for the blind, away from prying eyes. Treves suspected that behind Joseph's wish to live among the blind lay the hope that he could find a female companion, someone who wouldn't scream at the sight of him.[7] As Treves noted in his memoirs years later:

> *"His bodily deformity had left unmarred the instincts and feelings of his years. He was amorous. He would have liked to have been a lover, to have walked with the beloved object in the languorous shades of some beautiful garden and to have poured into her ear all the glowing utterances that he had rehearsed in his heart…imagine the feelings of such a youth when he saw nothing but horror*

creep over the face of every girl whose eyes met his."[8]

In an article written for the British Medical Journal in 1886, the surgeon stated bluntly that Merrick's genitals were *"perfectly normal,"* and the clinical photographs taken on his admission to the London Hospital confirm this.[9] Treves suspected that Joseph *"fell in love with every attractive woman he met,"*[10] and *"pictured himself the hero of many a passionate incident."*[11]

The frustration and loneliness Merrick must have experienced has sparked numerous fictional works on that theme, most notably, the Broadway play, *The Elephant Man,* (not related to the film), by Bernard Pomerance. Unlike the film, Pomerance's Treves is portrayed as a stern, prudish saviour of a poor and eternally grateful soul, quick to squelch Merrick's longing for closeness with another human being. Despite the trappings of fine clothes, a silver tea set and a library of books, Pomerance seems to say, Merrick will never be treated as fully human, yet in one of the most poignant lines of the play, Merrick (called John in the play) shows his staunch belief that his sufferings will not last forever:

> *"I believe in heaven. The Bible promises us in heaven, the crooked shall be made straight."*[12]

Treves introduced him to women who would treat him as a normal man, even a friend, as he had no doubt instructed them to do. Several months later, he asked Mrs. Leila Maturin, a *"young and pretty widow,"* according to him, to enter Joseph's room, shake his hand and wish him good morning without screaming or acting horrified. She did as Treves asked, and Joseph broke down. He wept uncontrollably. Treves wasn't surprised to learn afterwards that this was the first time Joseph had ever shaken hands with a woman.[13]

In the meantime, Joseph needed skilled care from hospital staff that wouldn't be fazed by his appearance. Along with Nurse

Ireland, Treves recruited more volunteer nurses to take care of his severe bronchitis and malnutrition after his harrowing travels to the Continent. Two years earlier, during his time with Tom Norman, Joseph had enjoyed *"appreciable good health and a fair amount of natural strength."*[14] Now he was greatly weakened and his heart was failing. A set of four photographs that Treves took showed a marked worsening of his condition since 1884.

After five months in the Isolation Ward, provided with free food and nursing care, Merrick needed a permanent home. Treves applied to The Royal Hospital For Incurables and the British Home For Incurables, but was turned down on both counts. He decided to enlist the help of the London Hospital Chairman, Francis Culling Carr-Gomm, who proved to be unexpectedly helpful.

Carr-Gomm wrote a letter to the Editor of the *London Times* describing Joseph's situation and appealed for help in funding his stay on a permanent basis.

> *"Sir:*
> *I am authorised to ask your powerful assistance in bringing to the notice of the public the following most exceptional case. There is now in a little room off one of our attic wards a man named Joseph Merrick, aged about twenty-seven* [sic, he was actually twenty-three], *a native of Leicester, so dreadful a sight that he is unable even to come out by daylight to the garden. He has been called "the elephant man" on account of his terrible deformity. I will not shock your readers with any detailed descriptions of his infirmities, but only one arm is available for work."*

Carr-Gomm summarised for the Times readers a brief outline of Joseph's life up until then, emphasising that, *"he has the greatest horror of the workhouse."* As with Tom Norman, Joseph did not hesitate to make his opinions known about his wretched life in the English Poor Law institution. It is to Carr-Gomm's eternal credit that he was able to step outside his bureaucratic boundaries and bend hospital rules on behalf of a suffering human being. In keeping with the Victorian morals that emphasised blamelessness and innocence in its victims, Carr-Gomm described Joseph's virtues and worthiness as a recipient of public charity:

> "...And that he is debarred from seeking to earn his livelihood in any ordinary way, yet he is superior in intelligence, can read and write, is quiet, gentle, not to say even refined in his mind..."

He highlighted Joseph's ability to make friends and his generosity of spirit: *"He occupies his time in the hospital by making with his one available hand little cardboard models, which he sends to the matron, doctor, and those who have been kind to him."*

Carr-Gomm demonstrates to us that he knew exactly how to capture sentimental Victorian hearts: *"Through all the miserable vicissitudes of his life, he has carried about a painting of his mother to show that she was a decent and presentable person."*

Interestingly, Treves's memoirs never mentioned Mary Jane's portrait. It's possible that he saw it or never took it seriously, having concluded that Mary Jane had abandoned Joseph to the workhouse at an early age. As we have seen, nothing could be further from the truth. Perhaps Joseph felt the need to conceal some part of his past from Treves.

In closing his letter, Carr-Gomm further stressed Joseph's being unable to work, as well as his pitiable fate:

> *"It is a case of singular affliction brought about through no fault of himself; he can but hope for quiet and privacy, during a life that Mr. Treves assures me is not likely to be long."*

The results were astonishing. The plight of *The Elephant Man* captured the imagination of the British public, and a flood of donations poured in. One of those generous donors named Mr. Singer, pledged fifty pounds a year for the rest of Joseph's life.

In December of 1886, Carr-Gomm received the approval of the Hospital Committee, to provide Joseph Merrick with a permanent home at the hospital. Admitting an 'incurable' to a hospital like the London was never heard of, but the Hospital Committee agreed that it would be inhumane to turn him out into the street again.

He became the London Hospital's most famous in-patient. Two rooms in a far wing were considered suitable, so the hospital's chief engineer, Mr. William Taylor, was brought in to refurbish them into a self-contained apartment. He converted one room into a comfortable bed-sit, where Joseph could receive company, and the other into a bathroom. Joseph needed daily baths to control his persistent skin odour.

Treves escorted him from his attic room down to his new home. Joseph responded with dazed gratitude, barely able to comprehend that he was home at last.[15]

Footnotes

[1] Jonathan Pereira, *The Elements of Materia Medica and Therapeutics* p. 78
"The London Hospital typically served thin gruel, bread and beer to patients with fever and congestion".
[2] Frederick Treves, *The Elephant Man and Other Reminiscences*
[3] Reginald Tuckett, Howell & Ford, *The True History of the Elephant Man*, p. 101
[4] Frederick Treves, *The Elephant Man and Other Reminiscences*
[5] Howell & Ford, *The True History of the Elephant Man* ibid. p.94
[6] ibid.p 94
[7] Frederick Treves, *The Elephant Man and Other Reminiscences*
[8] ibid.
[9] Pathological Society of London, December 1886
[10] Frederick Treves, *The Elephant Man and Other Reminiscences*
[11] ibid.
[12] Bernard Pomerance, *The Elephant Man*, 1977
[13] Frederick Treves, *The Elephant Man and Other Reminiscences*
[14] Howell & Ford, *The True History of the Elephant Man*: Francis Carr-Gomm's Letter to the London Times, Dec. 1885
[15] Howell & Ford, *The True History of the Elephant Man*

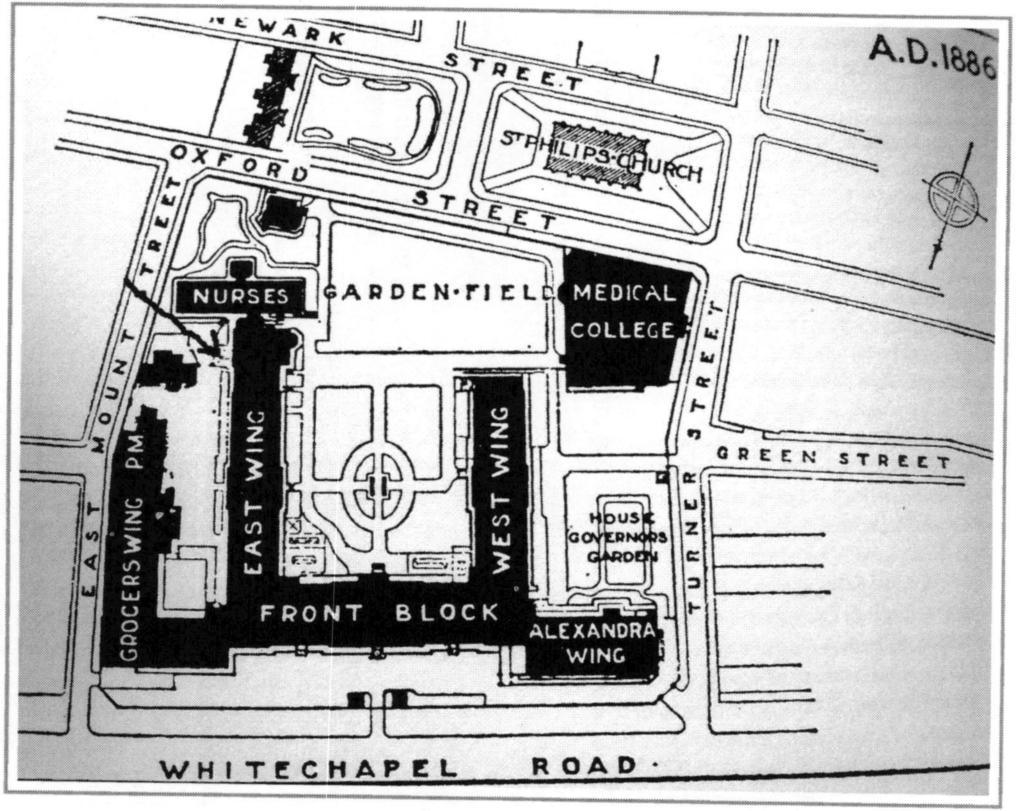

Layout of the London Hospital, Whitechapel, in 1886. This was the year Joseph was admitted. Bedstead Square, his final home, is marked by the arrow.

There is now only one garden at the hospital, but in the 1880s, there were three. Two public gardens and one reserved for Hospital governors. Prior to Garden Field, a cemetery occupied the spot. next to the Medical College. (Public domain)

The disguise Joseph Merrick wore, to hide his deformity. (The Royal London Hospital Archives & Museum. Copyright. All rights reserved).

Tom Norman, Joseph's London Manager. His Whitechapel exhibition was across the road from the London Hospital, where several doctors came to see him, including Frederick Treves.
(Leicester Mercury)

Tom Norman's sideshow. Although the photograph is in monochrome, this large attraction is vividly painted.
(Charmaine Troup. all rights reserved 2011. Copyright 2012)

Joseph Merrick in 1884, before presenting him to the London Pathological Society (believed to be sketch by Frederick Treves) (Public domain)

Liverpool Street Station, where Joseph arrived after a disastrous tour of the Continent in June, 1886. His money stolen and starving, he was mobbed by a crowd, as poignantly reenacted in the 1980 film, *The Elephant Man*. (public domain)

A view of 19th century Whitechapel and the London Hospital. The new Grocer's wing stands to the left of the clock.
(The Illustrated London News)

Rare views. Although the Royal London Hospital's Isolation Ward, (where Joseph was first given shelter), is long gone; a kind Hospital trustee gave the FoJCM a guided tour of nearby areas. They climbed this staircase and in a room off the corridor, was the Hospital's clock room. With many thanks to the Royal London Hospital. (Jeanette Sitton and Audrey Kantrowitz. Copyright 2012. All rights reserved).

67

Chapter 8

ANGELS OF MERCY

Joseph's new home was a basement apartment in the east wing, just below a courtyard. This area was nicknamed 'Bedstead Square' because it was used for cleaning, repairing and repainting old hospital bed frames, or bedsteads. Nonetheless, its seclusion from the rest of the hospital gave Joseph the privacy he had craved and a home he had longed for.

Gradually Joseph grew more confident and eager to talk. He would catch the odd glimpse of things going on upstairs in the square and made friends with workmen, proudly showing them the latest gifts from his many admirers.[1]

Other friendships came his way as well. William Taylor, the hospital engineer,[2] had a young son named Charles Edward. Charles would visit and play his violin for Joseph, and the two became close friends.

Also, though she apparently never met him in person, the eminent actress Madge Kendal became a generous benefactor, sending Joseph many gifts. These included a signed portrait, a gramophone and a beautiful cardboard model of Mainz Cathedral in Germany, which he assembled as a gift for her. (For a fascinating glimpse into the complexity of these models, which Joseph constructed, perhaps with the help of nurses, see the essay by Reverend Thomas Clay in Appendix D.)

Joseph had hoped Mrs. Kendal would come to pick it up so he could meet her, but William Kendal, her husband, came instead. The beautifully preserved model cathedral can be seen today, in the Archive Museum of the Royal London Hospital.

The closest people to Joseph were the nurses who took daily care of him, and of that group, Emma Ireland knew him the best.[3] Emma had just completed her nursing training the day Treves admitted Joseph in 1886.[4] Two years later she was promoted to Ward Sister (nurse in charge) of the Blizzard Ward. On the day Joseph died, she was the last nurse to see him alive. Two months after his death, she travelled to Hong Kong to care for plague patients. Tragically, she contracted bubonic plague and died on May 5, 1898. She and another Ward Sister were posthumously awarded the Hong Kong Plague Medal, the highest honour bestowed by the military on civilians.[5]

Joseph arrived at the London Hospital at a fortuitous time in its nursing history, when its nurses were well-trained in patient care under Matron Eva Luckes. According to the Nursing Service records of the Royal London Hospital:

"Before 1880, nurse probationers' training at the London Hospital consisted of one year's work on the wards, without examination, after which they were considered to be trained nurses. They were then expected to undertake a further two years service. A radical reorganisation of the nursing service was carried out in 1880, associated with the appointment of Eva Luckes as Matron, and the appointment of a subcommittee to review the system in 1879. After the reforms of 1880 it was established that a probationer's training should last 2 years, the first year being concerned with theoretical knowledge and the second with practical skills. If successful in the examination at the end of this time, the qualified nurse was expected to serve for a further year. The training was later extended to 3 years and 1 year after qualification. In 1884 a class of paying probationers for those who could afford to pay for their training, was introduced."[6]

The hospital staff who volunteered to care for Joseph had to go out of their way to reach him in Bedstead Square. Armed with bath supplies, linens, medicines and meal trays, they made the trek several times a day. His bronchitis now required constant attention and his shattered nerves made him frightened and wary of being touched.[7]

Frederick Treves certainly deserves credit for having given Joseph a permanent home, but he couldn't have kept him alive without the skilful care of the nurses. When they could spare the time, these compassionate women even brought cardboard models from a toy shop and helped Joseph assemble them.[8]

Despite the attention lavished on him, Joseph remained humble. When Treves published a medical article on Joseph's case in the Pathological Society's Transactions, Merrick eagerly added his own special note of gratitude:

> *"I should like to say a few words of thanks to all those that came forward with help and sympathy after my case was made known by Mr. Carr-Gomm in the public press."*[9]

Joseph was well aware that the hospital governor and committee had bent the rules *"...in letting me stay here till something definite was done concerning me, as the London Hospital is not a place where patients are kept permanently, although the Committee have made arrangements for me to do so."*[10]

After thanking several benefactors, he added, *"And lastly, my kind doctor, Mr. Treves, whose visits I greatly prize, as many more in the hospital do besides me. He is both friend and doctor to me. I have a nice bright room, made cheerful with flowers, books, and pictures."* In an echo of his 'Autobiography' pamphlet, Joseph concluded, *"I am very comfortable, and I may say as happy as my condition will allow me to be."* He finished by quoting from *False Greatness,* the poem by Isaac Watts that meant so much to him, which he also included in his show pamphlet.

His rooms came at a price though, and he paid rent in a form that was not always to his liking. Treves had examined him and photographed him on his arrival in 1886, charting the course of his deteriorating condition. The surgeon continued to examine him regularly and occasionally brought colleagues to view him as well. Joseph had to be available to be displayed and discussed at any time[11], yet Treves seemed to despise the showmen who had done the same in a far less humiliating way. From time to time, Joseph asked, *"Why can't I go back to Mr. Norman?"*[12], but that was no longer an option. His illness now required full time care. When his uncle Charles offered to take Joseph back, it was decided that his need of frequent baths made that an "obstacle."[13]

In these later years, Joseph's left hip gave him constant pain and Treves was dismayed to see that his head now measured the circumference of his waist.[14] It had grown so heavy that he could not lie down to sleep, without risking *"waking up with a broken neck,"* as he had wryly remarked to Tom Norman.[15] At night he was forced to sleep sitting up, supported by a pile of pillows behind his back. As Treves had told Carr-Gomm, Joseph's remaining days were, *"not likely to be long."*[16]

Having met Joseph's immediate physical needs, Treves set about to meet his patient's emotional needs as well. He brought a steady stream of well-prepared visitors to meet Joseph for tea or sit down for a quick chat, though he often had to act as interpreter. The growths in and around Joseph's mouth impeded his speech, and it took time for those around him to learn what he was saying.[17] Still, Leila Maturin's visit gave Joseph some much-needed self-confidence, and he became cheerfully conversant with subsequent visitors. They often brought books and signed photographs for his mantelpiece. Soon Joseph's apartment resembled that of a popular tenor of his day.[18]

On 21 May, 1887, the Prince and Princess of Wales came to open quarters for the nurses, to be called the Alexandra Home.[19] After

71

a ceremony of songs, blessings and speeches, the royal party visited the Medical College and several wards. One witness related that Princess Alexandra seemed much moved by the suffering she saw. She pulled flowers from her bouquet and gave them to the patients she spoke to. At her request, Frederick Treves accompanied the royal party to Bedstead Square to meet Joseph Merrick.

As always, Treves forewarned the visitors about Merrick's appearance. To Joseph's amazement and delight, Princess Alexandra greeted him with a gracious smile and a handshake. She sat down and chatted with him for a quarter of an hour, expressing great interest in his assortment of knickknacks and curios.[20] The Prince of Wales was amused to spot a signed photograph of Madge Kendal, a famous actress, on Merrick's mantelpiece.[21]

The excitement wasn't over. Several days later, a signed photograph of Alexandra arrived from Marlborough House to be added to Joseph's collection. He was so touched that he wept over it, and could hardly bear to let anyone else touch it, even Treves. The photograph was *"framed and hung in his room, almost as an icon."* Joseph wrote a letter of thanks to Alexandra that began *"My dear Princess..."* Touched by Joseph's heartfelt gratitude, Treves had the letter mailed despite the unorthodox form of address.[22]

It did no harm. At Christmas, Alexandra sent not one but three inscribed cards. She returned to visit several times. Soon it became fashionable to visit *The Elephant Man*. Several noble visitors became close friends, including Mrs. Welsley, Lady Dorothy Neville and Lady Louisa Knightley, who would help fulfil Joseph's wish to visit the countryside. 1887 was a good year for Joseph, despite his deteriorating condition.

But the best was yet to come.

Footnotes

[1] Howell & Ford, *The True History of the Elephant Man*, p. 113
[2] ibid, p.95
[3] Jonathan Evans, Archivist, Royal London Hospital
[4] http://becklibrary.org/GuthrieJournal/68_3_99/109_11.pdf
[5] http://www.mortonandeden.com/reports/r03_10_03.pdf
[6] http://www.aim25.ac.uk/cgi-in/vcdf/detail?coll_id=3909&inst_id=23
[7] Howell & Ford, *The True History of the Elephant Man*, p. 94
[8] ibid p. 95
[9] Pathological Society *Transactions,* 1886 p.180
[10] ibid.
[11] Howell & Ford, *The True History of the Elephant Man*, p. 140
[12] ibid, p.153
[13] ibid. p. 98
[14] Frederick Treves, *The Elephant Man and Other Reminiscences*
[15] Tom Norman's memoirs, *The Penny Showman,* The British Museum.
[16] Francis Carr-Gomm, letter to the London Times, December 1886, p. 93
[17] Frederick Treves, *The Elephant Man and Other Reminiscences*
[18] ibid
[19] Howell & Ford, *The True History of the Elephant Man*, p. 115
[20] ibid p. 116
[21] ibid p.116
[22] ibid p.117

LEFT: Francis Culling Carr-Gomm, the Hospital Chairman who lobbied on Joseph's behalf for a permanent home at the London Hospital. RIGHT: Sir Frederick Treves, Joseph's physician.

Princess Alexandra visits the London Hospital on May 23, 1878. After opening the new Alexandra Wing and visiting the general wards, she and the Prince of Wales paid a special visit to Joseph. She presented him with an autographed portrait, one of his greatest treasures.
(Jeanette Sitton, FoJCM. Copyright 2012. All rights reserved)

The door and window of Joseph's home in Bedstead Square (now demolished).

In the 1970s, the rooms were knocked through to form part of the Hospital's catering wing. The door and window in this picture were bricked up. (Public domain)

The steps that led down from Bedstead Square to Joseph's two adjoining rooms. Photo taken in 2005. (Jeanette Sitton, FoJCM. Copyright 2012. All rights reserved).

TOP: The hospital garden. This is where Joseph took walks at night, being unable to walk freely during the day. (Rebecca Timmons, FoJCM. Copyright 2012. All rights reserved).

BOTTOM: Much of the original 19th century hospital has been redeveloped in recent years, including Bedstead Square. (Carol Bassi. Copyright 2012. All rights reserved).

The distinguished actress, Dame Madge Kendal, Joseph's friend and patron. She sent him many gifts and sponsored his known trip to Drury Lane Theatre. However, they probably never met in person, though he hoped she would come to receive the model church he constructed for her. (Photo: public domain)

Joseph's armchair, coloured dark and light green, was specially designed for him by William Taylor, the hospital engineer who also outfitted his rooms with a bath and bed-sitting room. Courtesy the Taylor family. (Jeanette Sitton, FoJCM. Copyright 2012. All rights reserved).

The card Cathedral that Joseph built. It was made from a kit, and is of Mainz Cathedral in Germany. (Audrey Kantrowitz, FoJCM. Copyright 2012. All rights reserved).

Mainz Cathedral kit. The exact same model that Joseph built. It was published before 1893 by Joseph Scholz, as part of the series 'Little Master Builder'. (Reverend Thomas Clay. Copyright 2012. All rights reserved)

Chapter 9

A CHRISTMAS TO REMEMBER

Christmas at the London Hospital was a spectacular holiday, thanks to the dedicated staff that spared no effort to bring holiday cheer to the patients. The nurses sang carols and hung wreaths, doctors carved elaborate turkey dinners, medical students put on puppet shows for the children, and even the ward maids and floor scrubbers were treated to a holiday dance and midnight supper.[1]

Christmas 1887 was unlike any other, beginning with Princess Alexandra's special holiday greetings. As noted, since her visit in May, many members of high society had followed in her wake.[2] Joseph's visitors came bearing signed portraits of themselves, flowers, and books, among other things. But no gift meant so much to Joseph as the one Treves bought for him at his request that year.

It was a gentleman's dressing case, fitted with silver grooming accessories. These consisted of a comb, hairbrush, toothbrush, hat brush, cigarette case, shoehorn, and mirror. They were the *"perfect props for Joseph's imagination."*[3] As he sat in his room opening and closing the case, neatly arranging each item on his table, he became a fashionable young *"man-about-town"* preparing for an evening out. Before presenting the gift to Joseph, Treves had made sure to remove the mirror. He also tactfully filled the cigarette case with cigarettes, even though Joseph couldn't actually hold one between his twisted lips.[4]

To add to the excitement, preparations were underfoot to fulfil one of Joseph's long-cherished dreams: to go to the theatre. Though he had read many plays, he had never been able to attend in person. The sight of him would no doubt raise a panic in the audience that would put a stop to any action on the stage.[5]

Philanthropist Baroness Burdett Coutts, a friend of actress Madge Kendall, kept a private box at Drury Lane Theatre. It was arranged for Joseph to see a traditional English pantomime. Though Treves does not give us the name of the show in his memoirs, it was most likely *Puss in Boots*.[6]

Puss in Boots was the ideal show for someone like Joseph, who had been compelled to draw on his imagination for much of life's experiences. His childlike aspect was awakened and dazzled by a show designed to dazzle and mesmerise the audience with a mix of colour, story, song, and dance.[7]

From his hidden seat in the borrowed box near the stage, Joseph could see all the action, while remaining unseen by the audience. Treves observed him closely:

> *"His reaction was not that so much of delight as of wonder and amazement. He was awed. He was enthralled. The spectacle left him speechless, so that if he were spoken to, he took no heed. He often seemed to be panting for breath - thrilled by a vision that was almost beyond his comprehension."*[8]

The pantomime would have closely followed the plot of the beloved fairy tale: when a miller dies, the only thing he leaves his youngest son is the family cat. But this is no ordinary cat. Puss in Boots is a clever companion who sets out to help the lad to seek his fortune. While the boy is swimming one day, Puss sees the royal coach coming and flags it down, crying that his master is drowning.

When rescued, the boy is introduced to the King, Queen, and Princess as the Marquis of Carabas. Of course, the Princess and the young lad fall in love at first sight. To win her, he must vanquish an ogre in a castle. Puss in Boots tricks the ogre into turning himself into a lion and then a mouse. Puss pounces on the mouse and puts an end to it in short order. Now his master is truly a wealthy lord of land and treasure. He wins the hand of the Princess and the tale ends happily ever after.[9]

Treves had enough insight to understand that despite his disfigurement, Joseph was like any other young man. Though impressed by the *"splendour and dignity"* of the production, the doctor observed that Merrick was even more captivated by *"the ladies of the ballet."*[10]

The doctor also noticed that Joseph was not amused, and perhaps was even disturbed, by the slapstick acts of clowns during the interval. But the entrance of a pompous policeman who was roundly set upon by the clowns caused Merrick to chuckle, perhaps in delighted revenge after having his own livelihood cut off by officious police in various towns.[11]

"As with the novels he read, every aspect of the show was real to him," documented Treves.

> "...the palace was the home of kings, the princess was of royal blood, and the fairies were as undoubted as the children in the street, while the dishes at the banquet were of unquestionable gold."[12]

> "'He did not like to discuss it as a play, but rather as a vision of some actual world. 'I wonder what the Prince did after we left?' he would ask, or, 'do you think that poor man is still in the dungeon?'"[13]

No matter how many novels or plays he had read, Joseph had always been forced to live on the edge of other people's lives, in isolation and loneliness. *"It was as if his disorder had forced him to become a bystander in the business of living, starving him of social relationships and of the most basic human experiences."*[14]

To compensate, he had created a complex fantasy world, peopled by heroic men and impossibly beautiful women. Though it's not certain whether he went to the theatre on several more occasions, there's no doubt that the night he saw *Puss in Boots* was the first time Joseph Merrick saw dreams come to life.

Footnotes

[1] Howell & Ford, *The True History of the Elephant Man*, p, 118
[2] *The Autobiography of Joseph Carey Merrick*, 174
[3] ibid, p. 51
[4] Howell & Ford, *The True History of the Elephant Man*, p. 56
[5] Frederick Treves, *The Elephant Man and Other Reminiscences*
[6] Howell & Ford, *The True History of the Elephant Man,* p. 119
[7] ibid, p. 119
[8] Howell & Ford, *The True History of the Elephant Man*, p, 121
[9] ibid. p. 122
[10] Frederick Treves, *The Elephant Man and Other Reminiscences*
[11] Howell & Ford, *The True History of the Elephant Man*, p, 121
[12] Frederick Treves, *The Elephant Man and Other Reminiscences*
[13] ibid
[14] ibid
[15] ibid
[16] Howell & Ford, *The True History of the Elephant Man*, p, 126
[17] *Politics and Society: The Journals of Lady Louisa Knightley 1885-1913*, Peter Gordon, ed

A gentleman's vanity case which probably looks similar to the one Joseph used. (Margi O'Neill, Serpentine Antiques. Copyright 2012. All rights reserved).

Chapter 10

FRESH AIR AND FREEDOM

Since his nightmarish journey home from Belgium in 1886, Joseph had not traveled often outside London. His outings consisted mainly of nightly strolls in the hospital's garden. On at least one occasion though, he was invited to visit Francis Carr-Gomm's estate. In his memoir, *All Things Considered,* Carr-Gomm's nephew, Richard, relates a touching anecdote of his uncle finding Joseph in a room alone, quietly reciting the Lord's Prayer. Joseph gave the Carr-Gomms one of his model churches. It remained on their mantelpiece for years until a maid knocked it to the floor whilst cleaning.

Frederick Treves observed that Merrick's severely restricted life sometimes made him *"hopelessly despondent."*[1] This warm-hearted young man lived essentially as a prisoner in his small apartment. Treves tells us that sometimes Joseph resorted to *"beating time on his pillow to some tune ringing in his head. I have many times found him so occupied when I entered his room unexpectedly."*[2] Rather than enjoyment of imaginary music, this self-stimulation can be seen as a *"classic depressive symptom."*[3]

Living in such confinement occasionally made Joseph so lonely that he wandered to the wards in search of company. The distracted nurses hastily bundled him back to his rooms before general pandemonium could break out.[4] One can only imagine what a painful reminder that must have been to Joseph, that there would always be a barrier between him and the rest of the world. On the other hand, Joseph had difficulty trusting that the London Hospital was his permanent home and refuge from disruption. Since childhood, his life had been marked by upheaval as his restless father moved the family from one home to another in the poor neighbourhoods of Leicester. Joseph had enjoyed two years of relative stability at his uncle's house, then four years of unremitting horror in the workhouse. When he expressed a desire to be moved to a lighthouse or a home for the blind, Joseph disclosed his lingering anxiety that he might be forced to reveal himself to hostile eyes. Treves found it difficult to convince *"this small and infinitely vulnerable man"*[5] that he no longer had to travel and perform for his room and board.

In caring for Joseph, Frederick Treves was ahead of his time. He understood that human contact was as essential to Joseph's mental health as food and care was to his mental needs. He tells us that in those years, he had time to visit Joseph daily (and insisted that his house surgeons do the same).[6] He also spent two hours with Joseph every Sunday morning, bringing him reading materials and learning to decipher his impeded speech. He discovered that Merrick possessed *"unguessed-at emotional depths"*[7] and a hunger for conversation. Joseph could be moved easily to compassion, grief, and sometimes even anger in certain situations. Most of his perceptions of humankind were formed from reading books, and, according to Treves, he longed to become a *"gallant young spark,"* a *"Piccadilly exquisite."*[8]

Other doctors noticed that tendency as well. Reginald Tuckett, wrote years later of Joseph's *"fascination with fine clothes"* and the *"pathetic pride he took in his normal left arm"*.[9] Another house doctor, Wilfred Grenfell, noticed the same dark sense of humour that Tom Norman remembered, when Joseph speculated on how he would look, *"preserved in a huge bottle of alcohol, a fate which in his imagination he was destined to become."*[10]

Joseph's chief passions were books and conversation, though he also enjoyed sketching and crafting models from cardboard kits. His most intricate one was probably the model given him by Madge Kendal. After completing it for her, he hoped he could present it to her in person. To his disappointment, she sent her husband instead. (Contrary to the tender scenes in the *Elephant Man* film and play, Mrs. Kendal probably never met Joseph in person.)[11] The beautiful church model has survived and is on display in the Royal London Hospital's Museum. It is truly a testimony to Joseph's patience and love of beauty.[12]

But eventually any diversion wears thin, and Joseph's bouts of melancholy grew more noticeable. Treves cast about for a way to send him on holiday to the countryside, where he had always longed to go. Lady Dorothy Neville, a writer and prominent horticulturalist, offered Joseph a cottage on her estate, but stipulated that Joseph remain indoors until dark. Treves decided this was unacceptable and contrary to the purpose of the outing.[13]

Into the breach stepped Lady Louisa Knightley, whose name well suited her. She was Lady of Fawsley Hall Manor, just outside Daventry in Northamptonshire. Lady Knightley took a keen interest in politics, and was an early advocate of women's suffrage. She had a strong sense of mission towards the poor, as well as a deep love for the *"intensely rural areas"* of the Midlands. She generously invited Joseph to stay in a cottage on her estate with no restrictions of when or where he could roam.[14]

As with any outing involving Joseph, an elaborate scheme had to be devised to avoid frightening the public. He was concealed in a carriage and taken to the train station, where a second class railroad car, reserved for his use, had been shunted into a siding. After he boarded it, the car was coupled to the rest of the train, allowing Joseph to travel in undisturbed solitude to Northampton.[15]

A local farmer met him at the station and drove him to his cottage, roughly forty minutes away by today's transport. Unfortunately, after all the elaborate efforts to avoid shocking anyone unawares, the farmer's wife, who had not been warned of her guest's appearance, screamed and fled into the woods. She declared herself *"all of a-twitter"* and utterly unable to host

Joseph. It must have been a cruel blow to his feelings, after seeking to escape precisely that type of reaction.[16]

A gamekeeper named Goldby and his wife offered their home at Red Hill Farm for the duration instead. The cottage stood a quarter of a mile from the woods and stream, close enough for Joseph to walk unsupervised while savouring the fresh country air. His sense of freedom must have been exhilarating. Lady Knightley came to visit while he was there, and wrote later in her diary that she had found Merrick quite comfortable with the Goldbys and, *"Merrick has such nice brown eyes, and I looked straight into them..."*[17]

Although Treves described Joseph's time in the country as his *"one supreme holiday,"* he actually visited Fawsley four times in total: 1887, 1888, and twice in 1889. In his memoirs, Treves calls up a vivid image of Joseph: *"the Merrick who had once crouched terrified in the filthy shadows of the Mile End shop [sic, Whitechapel]... was now sitting in the sun, in a clearing among the trees, arranging a bunch of violets he had gathered."*

One can only feel gratitude towards the surgeon for making sure Joseph knew moments of pure happiness before the end.

Footnotes

[1] Carr-Gomm, Richard *All Things Considered* (Trafford Publishing (July 15, 2005)
[2] Frederick Treves, *The Elephant Man And Other Reminiscences*
[3] Howell &Ford, *The True History of the Elephant Man*, p. 106
[4] ibid. p. 113
[5] ibid. p. 107
[6] ibid. p. 100
[7] ibid, p.104
[8] ibid, p 119
[9] Ibid. 101.
[10] ibid p.101
[11] ibid..p.111
[12] Howell &Ford, *The True History of the Elephant Man*, plate .28
[13] *Dame Madge Kendal's Memoirs*
[14] Howell &Ford, *The True History of the Elephant Man*, p. 142
[15] ibid. p.142
[16] Howell &Ford, *The True History of the Elephant Man*, p. 143
[17] *Politics and Society: The Journals of Lady Louisa Knightley*, 1885-1913, Peter Gordon, ed.

Chapter 11

PEACE AT LAST

One of Joseph's favourite activities was writing notes to his many well-wishers. When he visited the countryside, a young man named Walter Steel came from a neighbouring farm every day to post the letters for him. In later years, Walter recalled that Joseph would sit just out of sight in the woods to write. Like Bertram Dooley, Joseph's friend and bodyguard in Sam Roper's Fair, Walter considered Joseph a *"well-educated"* man with many interesting things to say.[1] Joseph took great delight in his natural surroundings. He wrote many letters to Frederick Treves, describing the birdcalls and the wildlife in the woods. He pressed flowers he had found, between the pages of the letters, and wrote proudly of making friends with a noisy, frightening dog.

The last known letter Joseph wrote was in October 1890 while at Fawsley Hall. It was addressed to Mrs. Leila Maturin, the first woman who, according to Treves, had shaken his hand in a friendly greeting. By now, Mrs. Maturin had returned to her native Scotland. From her home on the Isle of Islay, she sent lovely gifts to Joseph, which he always appreciated. The letter survives and can be seen in the Royal Hospital Archives Museum in London. It was composed on a single sheet of stationery decorated with an 18th century couple in formal dress. Joseph's left-handed script is astonishingly graceful, yet there is an interesting discrepancy in the fact that he addresses Mrs. Maturin as *"Miss."* He knew quite well she was a widow.

> *"Dear Miss Maturin,*
> *Many thanks indeed for the grouse and the books you so kindly sent me. The grouse were splendid. I saw Mr. Treves on Sunday—he said I was to give his best regards to you. With much gratitude I am yours truly,*
> *Joseph Merrick, London Hospital, Whitechapel"*

It's still a mystery as to how Treves met Leila Maturin in London. She was born Leila Scot Skirving and grew up on a farm with her three brothers, Owen and Archibald. After the death of her mother, her father brought the family to Edinburgh where Leila become a delightful figure in the social scene. As a girl, she charmed Robert Louis Stevenson and participated in theatrical evenings and musicals. One of her brothers, Archibald, became a distinguished artist. Another brother, Robert Scot Skirving, travelled to Australia and served there as a surgeon for many years. Perhaps Leila Maturin's connection with Treves was through Leslie Maturin, her husband from Dublin. He was a young doctor whose research on a form of curare, a (muscle relaxant) proved to be very helpful in treating tetanus spasms. He and Leila had only been married for three months when he treated a child with scarlet fever and came down with the disease himself. Within twenty-four hours, he had passed away. Leila never remarried. She was thirty-one at the time she was introduced to Joseph Merrick. Eventually, she left London and returned to Edinburgh, where she became notable for her charity work and a prominent member of many organisations, including Scotland's early National Geographic Society. Immortalised by Treves as the *"young and pretty widow"* who gave Joseph Merrick a handshake that would change his life forever, Leila Maturin died in 1913 at the age of 62 and was buried next to her husband in Dublin.[2]

On returning to Bedstead Square, Joseph's condition continued to deteriorate. His heart was considerably weaker and his episodes of bronchitis were becoming more frequent. The tumour that had been removed from his mouth in the Leicester Infirmary had begun to grow again, interfering with his speech and eating. His head had grown so large he could barely hold it up. Treves wondered how much longer he could go on.[3]

As an avid reader of the Bible, Joseph began to meet with the hospital's chaplain, Reverend Tristan Valentine. He expressed a desire to be confirmed in the Anglican faith, though it was quite different from his mother's Baptist church. Reverend Valentine came up with an ingenuous way for Joseph to attend Sunday services. He was allowed to sit in the vestry where he could worship and take Communion without being seen by the congregation during Sunday services.

On Easter Sunday, 6 April, 1890, Joseph attended not one but two early morning services.[4] During the next few days he pursued his normal routine of reading, writing letters, receiving visitors and taking evening walks in the hospital garden. On Friday, 11 April, Joseph remained in bed until late morning, as was his custom these days. He had most likely gone for a walk in the garden the night before, and needed the extra rest. Treves had observed that he had become like a feeble old man these days, wizened and weak.[5]

At noon, Nurse Emma Ireland came to attend to Joseph's needs. As we have seen, she had been his nurse since the early days in the Isolation Ward. Recently she had been promoted to Head Sister of Blizzard Ward, but she continued to visit Joseph. That day, she spoke to him as usual and left him sitting up comfortably in bed.

Emma Ireland was the last nurse to see Joseph Merrick alive. At 1.30pm, a ward maid brought Joseph's lunch and left it for him to eat in his own time. At 3.00pm, Dr. Ashe, one of Treves's attending surgeons, came for a routine visit and found Joseph lying flat across his bed. The young doctor knew Joseph always needed to sleep sitting up. He saw at once that Merrick was dead. As Dr. Ashe testified later in the inquest, he *"felt so shaken he didn't touch the body."*

Instead, he sought a senior surgeon, Dr. Hodges, and they examined Joseph's body before notifying Frederick Treves.[6] The cause of death was ruled to be *"asphyxiation,"* stating that the windpipe was crushed by the weight of the head. In his memoirs, however, Treves theorised that Joseph had died of a broken neck, perhaps from trying deliberately to sleep *"like normal people."* Though it could be argued that Treves knew Joseph better than anyone, the results of the report remained *"asphyxiation."* It's also possible that since he was found lying across the bed, Joseph might have suffered a heart attack or stroke while trying to get up. Thus he would have fallen over backwards accidentally.[7]

In March of 2011, a team of international researchers and CGI (computer graphics imaging) specialists gathered in London to investigate the circumstances of Joseph's death and recreate how he might have walked and talked. These experts included osteoarchaeologist, Rose Drew; ear, nose and throat surgeon, John Rubin; spinal trauma expert, Alex Vaccaro; and speech and language therapist, Ruth Epstein.[8]

The CGI specialists from France, headed by Benjamin Moreno, analysed Joseph's warped bones with a special light scanner. For two days they studied every part of his preserved skeleton and created a digital copy, which they taught to walk through over 30,000 hours of computer simulation. While the main focus of the investigation was to determine the circumstances of his death, speech pathologists Rubin and Epstein worked with an actor to simulate Joseph's constricted speech.

Alex Vaccaro and Rose Drew discovered that there was damage to the highest cervical vertebrae in Joseph's spine (called $C1$-$C2$.) They concluded that Joseph's death was indeed accidental, not intentional. According to Dr. Vaccaro, *"When you lean back, your reflexes cause you to startle and change position, just like you can't drown yourself."*

As Merrick's head tipped back, the weight of it caused compression to the vertebral arteries and the spinal cord. According to Dr. Vaccaro, the damaged nervous tissue around the brain and spinal cord caused Joseph to suffer a stroke and become instantly paralysed. Vaccaro concludes, *"You can't wake up from that."*[9]

We can only hope that Joseph's final moments of his short life were peaceful.

Treves took charge of the body and dissected it. He called for tissue samples to be taken, and commissioned plaster casts of Joseph's head, right arm, and foot. Later, the skeleton was cleaned and articulated by Thomas Horrocks Openshaw, Curator of the London Hospital's Pathology Museum. The brass plate, at the foot of the skeleton reads, in capital letters, "THE ELEPHANT MAN".

In 2012, a replica of the skeleton was created from digital 3D scans of his fragile remains. It stands in the Hospital's museum.

Yet even as Joseph became a specimen for the ages, it would not be too far-fetched to recall Tom Norman's introduction of the *Elephant Man* before each show. As part of his stage patter, Norman declared Joseph Merrick to be, *"probably the most remarkable human being ever to draw the breath of life."*

Footnotes

[1] Howell & Ford, *The True History of the Elephant Man*, p. 145
[2] http://www.maturin.org.uk/6.html
[3] Frederick Treves, *The Elephant Man and Other Reminiscences*
[4] Howell & Ford, *The True History of the Elephant Man*, p. 145
[5] ibld. p. 146
[6] Jonathan Evans, curator, The Royal London Archives Museum
[7] *Meet the Elephant Man*, Windfall Films, Discovery Networks of Europe UK, first aired March 29, 2011
[8] ibid.
[9] ibid

EPILOGUE

A commemorative plaque for Joseph Merrick

In 2003, the Friends of Joseph Carey Merrick, (FoJCM), launched a website appeal, asking for donations to create a commemorative plaque. Glenn Andrews, a Leicester Stonemason heard about it and very kindly donated his services and materials to create one for us. We sent him the wording and once the granite had arrived from Asia, (especially imported for the job), work began. *"It was a labour of love"*, Glenn said. The deeply set, gold leaf inscription reads:

"Joseph Carey Merrick, Son of Leicester, 1862-1890. A true model of bravery and dignity for all peoples of all generations. Erected by his Friends, worldwide, in 2004".

On 16th May, 2004, the plaque was fixed to the wall of the Gaiety Theatre building, at the corner of Leicester's Gladstone Street and Wharf Street South. The unveiling was by the Lord Mayor of Leicester, Cllr. Ramnik Kavia. Sadly, not long afterwards, it went missing. The building was due to be demolished and the developer, not wanting the memorial to become damaged, took it into safekeeping. Audrey Kantrowitz and Jeanette Sitton (both FoJCM), collected the plaque and it was later presented to the Moat Community College by Stephen Butt (FoJCM). It is now on the wall next to the reception.

Moat Community College
There is a historic connection between the Moat Community College and Joseph. The college stands on what was once the Leicester Union Workhouse, where Joseph was an inmate for a few years. An unpleasant association? Actually no, the college is

a central, prominent place of learning and educates teenagers against discrimination of all kinds, including: race; religious beliefs and disabilities. We think Joseph would have approved.

Handing over of the plaque to the Moat Community College, Leicester. Left to right: Stephen Butt (FoJCM); Student Council chairman Habiburrehman Kara and Jeanette Sitton, (FoJCM). (Leicester Mercury)

SIGNIFICANT DATES

1853, Feb 15: Frederick Treves, born
1861, Dec 29: Joseph Rockley Merrick weds Mary Jane Potterton, Thurmaston England
1862, Aug 5: Joseph Carey Merrick, born at 50, Lee Street, Leicester England
1864, Apr 21: John Thomas Merrick, born
1864, Jul 24: John Thomas dies from variola (smallpox) and is buried in Welford Road Cemetery, Leicestershire
1865: Merricks move to 119, Upper Brunswick Street
1866, Jan: William Arthur Merrick, born
1867, Sept 28: Marion Eliza Merrick, born
1868: Merricks move to 161, Birstall Street/Russell Square
1870, Dec 21: William Arthur Merrick dies from scarlet fever and is buried in Welford Road Cemetery, Leicestershire
1870: Charles Barnabas Merrick opens a Barber / Tobacco / Umbrella repair shop at 144 Churchgate, Leicester
1871: Frederick Treves begins medical studies at the London Hospital, London England
1873, May 19: Mary Jane Merrick. (Joseph's mother) dies from bronchial-pneumonia and is buried with William Arthur and Potterton siblings in Welford Road Cemetery, Leicestershire
1874: Merricks move to 4, Wanlip Street
1874, Dec 3: Joseph Rockley Merrick weds Emma Wood Antill at the Baptist Church of Archdeacon Lane
1874-75: Merricks move to 37, Russell Square
1875: Joseph Merrick finds work at Messrs. Freeman Cigar Factory, 9 Lower Hill Street. He is forced to relinquish employment due to the increasing overgrowth of his right hand
1877: Joseph Merrick begins short-lived work as a door-to-door salesman
1877: Joseph Merrick moves in with Uncle Charles; Aunt Jane and Grandmother Sarah Rockley Merrick, over the barber shop

1879, Dec 29: Joseph Merrick meets with William Cartwright, administrator of the Leicester Workhouse and is admitted.
1879: Dr. Frederick Treves becomes a surgeon at the London Hospital
1880, Mar 22: Joseph Merrick leaves the workhouse after a six week stay
1880, Mar 24: Joseph Merrick returns, destitute, to the workhouse
1882: Dr. Frederick Treves publishes his first book entitled 'Scrofula and Glandular Disease'
Mid- 1882: Joseph Merrick undergoes surgery at Leicester Union Infirmary to remove a fleshy protuberance from his upper lip. Dr. Charles Marriott and Dr. Thomas Warburton Benfield are presumed to have attended.
1884: Dr. Frederick Treves is appointed Head Surgeon of London Hospital
1884, Aug 29: Joseph Merrick eats his final meal at workhouse
1884, Aug: Joseph Merrick begins his career as a sideshow freak with entrepreneur Sam Torr and a consortium of Midlands showmen, acting as the Elephant Man's managers/agents.
1884, Nov: Dr. Frederick Treves visits the Elephant Man exhibit at 123, Whitechapel Road, London, England.
1884, Dec 2: Frederick Treves presents Merrick to the London Pathological Society, at 53, Berners Street, Bloomsbury, England.
1885, Mar 17: Frederick Treves makes his second presentation to the London Pathological Society. This time, Joseph Merrick is not present.
1886, June: Joseph Merrick is robbed and abandoned by a Showman named Farrari, while in Brussels, Belgium.
1886, June: Joseph Merrick arrives at Liverpool Street railway station, London, England
1886, Dec 4: Francis Culling Carr-Gomm, Chairman of the London Hospital, writes a letter to the London Times outlining Merrick's case.
1887, May 21: Joseph Merrick receives a visit from Alexandra, Princess of Wales and the Duke of Cambridge

1887: Joseph Merrick attends a theatrical performance at Drury Lane Theatre.
1888: New photos of Joseph Merrick document the disease's rapid progress
1889: Joseph Merrick enjoys a holiday at Fawsley Estate, Northampton England (one of four holidays to this place)
1890, Apr 6: Joseph Merrick attends both Easter services in the London Hospital Chapel
1890, Apr 11: Joseph Carey Merrick dies some time between 1.30 pm and 3 pm at London Hospital. The body is found by Mr. Hodges and Mr. Ashe.
1890, Apr 15: Mr. Wynne Baxter, (coroner), leads a judicial inquiry into Merrick's death. The cause of death is ruled as asphyxiation due to his head crushing his windpipe.
1890, Apr 16: Francis Carr-Gomm writes letter to the London Times detailing Merrick's life and death
1890, Apr: Joseph Merrick's remains are cast in plaster, specimens are taken, and the body is dissected by Dr. Frederick Treves. The skeleton is cleaned and articulated by T. H. Openshaw, Curator of the London Hospital's Pathology Museum, and housed at the Royal London Hospital's Medical College. <u>It is not on display to the public.</u>
1891: Marion Eliza Merrick (Joseph's sister) dies from mylitis and "seizures." She is buried in Belgrave Cemetery, Leicestershire
1897, Jan 30: Joseph Rockley Merrick (Joseph's father) dies from chronic bronchitis and is buried with Marion Eliza Merrick in Belgrave Cemetery
1898: Dr. Frederick Treves declines a Consulting Physician post at the London Hospital
1899: Dr. Frederick Treves serves as physician during the Boer War in South Africa.
1900: Dr. Frederick Treves is discharged from duty after being stricken with distemper

1901: Dr. Frederick Treves performs a successful appendicectomy on Edward VII two days before his coronation. He receives a baronetcy from King.

1922: Sir Frederick Treves publishes final book, *The Elephant Man and Other Reminiscences,* Cassell, 1922

1923, Dec 7: Sir Frederick Treves dies from peritonitis in Switzerland, aged 70.

1924, Jan 2: Sir Frederick Treves' funeral service was at St. Peter's Church, Dorchestershire and his ashes buried at Fordington cemetery, Dorchester, (England).

Fawsley Hall Estate, the private estate of Lady Louisa Knightley, who sponsored three holidays for Joseph on her estate. The Manor is now a hotel. (Fawsley Hall Hotel. Copyright 2012. All rights reserved.)

Red Hill Farm, where Joseph stayed in the Autumn of 1889 (Emma-Jane Hartley. Copyright 2012. All rights reserved).

Lady Louisa Knightley (Public domain).

ABOVE: St. Mary the Virgin church, inside the Fawsley Hall grounds. (Common License. Wikipedia).

LEFT: Alabaster vault of Sir Richard Knightley and wife Jane Skenard, heiress to Old Aldington. c1540. (Walwyn, Flickr. Commons License).

As a religious man, Merrick may have visited this church, while on holiday.

SUPPLEMENTAL ARTICLES

The Autobiography of Joseph Carey Merrick

I first saw the light on the 5th of August, 1860; I was born in Lee Street, Wharf Street, Leicester. The deformity which I am now exhibiting was caused by my mother being frightened by an Elephant; my mother was going along the street when a procession of Animals were passing by, there was a terrible crush of people to see them, and unfortunately she was pushed under the Elephant's feet, which frightened her very much; this occurring during a time of pregnancy was the cause of my deformity.

The measurement around my head is 36 inches, there is a large substance of flesh at the back as large as a breakfast cup, the other part in a manner of speaking is like hills and valleys, all lumped together, while the face is such a sight that no one could describe it. The right hand is almost the size and shape of an Elephant's foreleg, measuring 12 inches round the wrist and 5 inches round one of the fingers; the other hand and arm is no larger than that of a girl ten years of age, although it is well proportioned. My feet and legs are covered with thick lumpy skin, also my body, like that of an Elephant, and almost the same colour, in fact, no one would believe until they saw it, that such a thing could exist. It was not perceived much at birth, but began to develop itself when at the age of 5 years.

I went to school like other children until I was about 11 or 12 years of age, when the greatest misfortune of my life occurred, namely - the death of my mother, peace to her, she was a good mother to me; after she died my father broke up his home and went to lodgings; unfortunately for me he married his landlady; henceforth I never had one moment's comfort, she having children of her own, and I not being so handsome as they, together with my deformity, she was the means of making my life a perfect misery; lame and deformed as I was, I ran, or rather walked away from home two or three times, but suppose father had some spark of parental feeling left, so he induced me to return home again. The best friend I had in those days was my father's brother, Mr. Merrick, hair Dresser, Church Gate, Leicester.

When about 13 years old, nothing would satisfy my stepmother until she got me out to work; I obtained employment at Messrs. Freeman's Cigar Manufacturers, and worked there about two years, but my right hand got too heavy for making cigars, so I had to leave them.

I was sent about the town to see if I could procure work, but being lame and deformed no one would employ me; when I went home for my meals, my stepmother used to say I had not been to seek for work. I was taunted and sneered at so that I would not go home for my meals, and used to stay in the streets with a hungry belly rather than return for anything to eat, what few half-meals I did have, I was taunted with the remark -- *"That's more than you have earned."*

Being unable to get employment my father got me a peddler's license to hawk the town, but being deformed, people would not come to the door to buy my wares. In consequence of my ill luck my life was again made a misery to me, so that I again ran away and went hawking on my own account, but my deformity had grown to such an extent, so that I could not move about the town without having a crowd of people gather around me. I then went into the infirmary at Leicester, where I remained for two or three years, when I had to undergo an operation on my face, having three or four ounces of flesh cut away; so thought I, I'll get my living by being exhibited about the country. Knowing Mr. Sam Torr, Gladstone Vaults, Wharf Street, Leicester, went in for

Novelties, I wrote to him, he came to see me, and soon arranged matters, recommending me to Mr. Ellis, Beehive Inn, Nottingham, from whom I received the greatest kindness and attention.

In making my first appearance before the public, who have treated me well -- in fact I may say I am as comfortable now as I was uncomfortable before. I must now bid my kind readers adieu."

Joseph Merrick
Source: Howell & Ford, "The True History of the Elephant Man"

"THE *ELEPHANT MAN*"
Medical article by Frederick Treves, New York Medical Abstract (1886) British Medical Journal, December 11th, 1886

The subject of the following sketches, John (sic) Merrick, was twice before the Path. Soc. of London, the last time in 1885, when the case was described as one of "Congenital Deformity." Since that time the disease has made great progress, until the condition represented in the accompanying illustrations has been reached.

The Elephant Man is a native of Leicester, and is about 27 years of age. He earned his living at one time by exhibiting himself under the name which he still bears – a name not meant to imply elephantiasis, but bestowed on him on account of the bony exostoses on his frontal bone. This, combined with a deformity of the superior maxilla, which gives a trunk-like appearance to the nose and upper lip, causes the profile of the face to remind the observer of the profile of an elephant's head.

He is short, and lame through old diseases of the left hip-joint. The integuments and the bones are deformed. The subcutaneous tissues are greatly increased in amount in certain regions, where the integument is consequently raised prominently above the surrounding skin. This tissue is very loose, so that it can be raised from the deeper parts in great folds. In the right pectoral region, at the posterior aspect of the right axilla, and over the buttocks, the affected skin forms heavy pendulous flaps.

The skin is also subject to papilloma, represented in some parts, as in the right clavicular region, by a mere roughening of the integument: over the right side of the chest, the front of the abdomen, the back of the neck, and over the right popliteal space, the growth is small; on the other hand, great masses of [p.465] papillomata cover the back and gluteal regions. The eyelids, the ears, the entire left arm, nearly the whole of the front of the abdomen, the right and left thigh, the left leg, and the back of the right leg. The genitals are normal.

The deformities of the osseous system are yet more remarkable. The cranial bones are deformed and overgrown, so that the circumference of the patient's head equals that of his waist. This deformity is better shown by the woodcuts than by any verbal descriptions. Bony exostoses spring from the frontal bone and posterior part of the parietals, and the occipital. Irregular elevations lie between these bones, and all these deformities are very unsymmetrical. The right superior maxillary bone is greatly and irregularly enlarged. The right side of the hard palate and the right upper teeth occupy a lower level than the corresponding parts of the left side. The nose is turned to the left and the lips are very prominent. A connective-tissue growth was removed four years ago from the upper jaw. All of the bones of the upper extremity, excepting the clavicle and scapula, and the bones of both feet, are hypertrophied, without exostoses.

The patient can give no family history of similar deformity, but declares that his mother was knocked down by an elephant in a circus when bearing him. The hypertrophy of the bones existed ever since he can remember the thickening of the skin and papillomatous growths were very trifling in degree of development in during childhood. The papillary excrescences are increasing rapidly, and hypertrophy of the integuments of the right hand is causing it to become slowly crippled. General health is good.

Sir Frederick Treves: A biography

Frederick Treves was born at 8 Cornhill, Dorchester, on the 15th of February, 1853. For two years he went to the school run by William Barnes, who became his life long mentor and whose influence never left him. Frederick completed his education at Merchant Taylors in London but was always hankering for the Dorset beyond the hills. He followed his brother into the medical profession. Treves commenced his medical studies at the London Hospital in 1867 and spent all of his professional life at that institution.

In 1901, Treves was appointed Sergeant Surgeon to King Edward VII. He performed a successful emergency appendicectomy on the king two days before his intended coronation. The following year Treves was honoured with a baronetcy.

While working at the London Hospital, Treves came across Joseph Merrick, who was exhibiting as *The Elephant Man* in a shop at 123 Whitechapel Road. Treves befriended Joseph Merrick and made his last years comfortable.

The doctor became a distinguished surgeon and prizewinning author of medical textbooks. At the age of fifty, Treves gave up his medical career to write several travel books. His last book though, *The Elephant Man and Other Reminiscences*, became his most famous. Treves retired to Switzerland with his wife, Anne (Mason). He died of peritonitis as a result of a ruptured appendix, his own field of specialty. His remains were cremated and brought back to England. His funeral was held at St Peter's church, Dorchester on 2 January 1924. Treves's close friend, author Thomas Hardy, (also from Dorset), wrote and delivered a poem at Fordington Cemetery. It was later published in The Times.

Publications:

- *Scrofula and its Gland Diseases* (London, 1882)
- *Surgical Applied Anatomy* (London, 1883)
- *Pathology, Diagnosis and Treatment of Obstruction of the Intestine* (London, 1884). Later revised and published as *Intestinal Obstruction, its Varieties with their Pathology, Diagnosis and Treatment* (1899).)
- *The Anatomy of the Intestinal Canal and Peritoneum* (London, 1885)
- *A Manual of Surgery* (3 vols, 1886)
- *A Manual of Operative Surgery* (1891)
- *The Student's Handbook of Surgical Operations* (London, 1892)
- *A System of Surgery* (edited by Treves) (2 vols, 1895)
- *Tale of a Field Hospital* (London, 1900)
- *Highways and Byways of Dorset* (1906)
- *The Cradle of the Deep* (1908)
- *Uganda for a Holiday* (1910)
- *The Land that is Desolate* (1912)
- *The Country of `The Ring and the Book'* (1913)
- *The Riviera of the Corniche Road* (1921)
- *Lake of Geneva* (1922)
- *The Elephant Man and Other Reminiscences* (1923)

Publications by others about Treves:
Sir Frederick Treves: The Extraordinary Edwardian, Stephen Trombley(London, 1989)

Sources:

The Joseph Carey Merrick Tribute Website, FoJCM
Sir Frederick Treves: The Extra-Ordinary Edwardian,
Stephen Trombley (London, 1989)
Obituary - Sir Frederick Treves', *British Medical Journal,* 1923, vol. ii, pp.1185-87 *Sir Frederick Treves: Surgeon, Author and Medical Historian*
Howell, Michael and Peter Ford, *The True History of the Elephant Man,* p. 161

Carr-Gomm's second letter to the Times, January 1887

To the editor of the Times:

Sir, - In a letter which you were kind enough to insert some weeks back about Joseph Merrick who had formerly exhibited under the name of "the Elephant Man" I asked whether any one could suggest a fitting home where he could be received, adding that I felt sure when such a home was found charitable people would come forward and enable me to place him therein. The letter interested many, and I received numerous kind answers from all parts of the country, and had my appeal been directly for money I am convinced abundance would have speedily been sent to me.

The practical result of the correspondence is that no home is to be found so suitable to his needs as the hospital, and we now feel ourselves justified in keeping him with us; and although a general hospital supported by voluntary contributions is strictly for curative purposes where each occupied bed represents an outlay little short of £70 per annum, our committee have decided under the peculiar circumstances, to set apart a small room where the poor fellow not only secures that privacy which is so essential to his comfort, but also is supplied with all that can possibly alleviate his sad condition, such as baths, good nursing, and medical supervision.

This is in accordance with the wishes expressed by most of the contributors, and Merrick himself, naturally enough, much prefers remaining where he has found so much sympathy and comfort.

If he leaves us, and he is of course a free agent, I shall now be able to provide for his being properly taken care of by an uncle at

Leicester, who is too poor a man to take him in unless means were given him, but there can be no question that he is far better off with us than he could possible be outside, and this is his own feeling.

As I have personally replied to each one who has written except, of course, anonymous contributors, I have not thought it necessary to publish any list, but I have received and hold in trust sufficient to enable me to provide for the poor fellow's comfort for some four or five years to come, and if more should then be required, I will ask for it.

As many have desired to know particulars of this unique case, I would add that some details are given, with illustrations, in the British Medical Journal of the 11th ultimo, one of our objects, however, is to prevent his deformity being made anything of a show, except for purely scientific purposes, and the hospital officials have instructions to secure for him as far as possible immunity from the gaze of the curious.

I have the honour to be, Sir, yours obediently,
F.C.CARR-GOMM, Chairman of the London Hospital.
London Hospital, Whitechapel-road, E.

APPENDIX A

WHAT IS PROTEUS SYNDROME?
An article by Dr. Leslie Biesecker, MD

National Institutes of Health
Dr. Leslie G. Biesecker, Chief, Genetic Disease Research Branch, NHGRI.

Proteus syndrome is an extremely rare overgrowth syndrome thought to affect fewer than 500 individuals in the developed world. It is characterised by the progressive and abnormal growth of body tissues, including skin, bones, fatty tissues and blood vessels. Physicians named the condition after the Greek god who could transform his shape. The most famous case of what some suggest could be Proteus syndrome is that of Joseph Merrick, known as *The Elephant Man*. Merrick gained celebrity — and for a time earned his livelihood in England and Europe — by being displayed in human novelty exhibitions as *The Elephant Man*.

He died in 1890 at the age of 27 in London Hospital, now the Royal London Hospital, where he resided at the end of his life. Merrick's life has been portrayed on stage, and in a 1980 Hollywood movie titled *"The Elephant Man."*

Medical literature through the 20th century contains other descriptions of the disorder. Canadian-based geneticist Michael Cohen, Jr., DMD, Ph.D., first described the condition in 1979, and Hans Rudolf Wiedemann, a German paediatrician gave the disease its name in 1983.

In July of 2011, a team led by researchers at the National Institutes of Health discovered that the genetic cause of the condition is a point mutation — a single-letter misspelling in the DNA of the genetic code — in the AKT1 gene that causes sporadic tissue growth. Unlike inherited genetic disorders, the gene variant that causes Proteus syndrome occurs spontaneously in each affected individual after conception in just one cell of the developing embryo. It is believed that the severity of the disease depends on when this spontaneous genetic change occurs in embryonic development. As the embryo grows and develops, only the descendants of the cell with the original AKT1 gene mutation display the hallmarks of the disease, leaving the individual with a mixture of normal and mutated cells, a condition called genetic mosaicism.

Newborns with Proteus syndrome almost always appear unaffected, and symptoms typically arise in the child's first two years of life. The mutation in AKT1 alters the ability of affected cells to regulate their own growth, causing some parts of the patient's body to grow to abnormal and even enormous sizes, while other parts of the body remain normal. The irregular overgrowth worsens with age and increases the susceptibility to tumours.

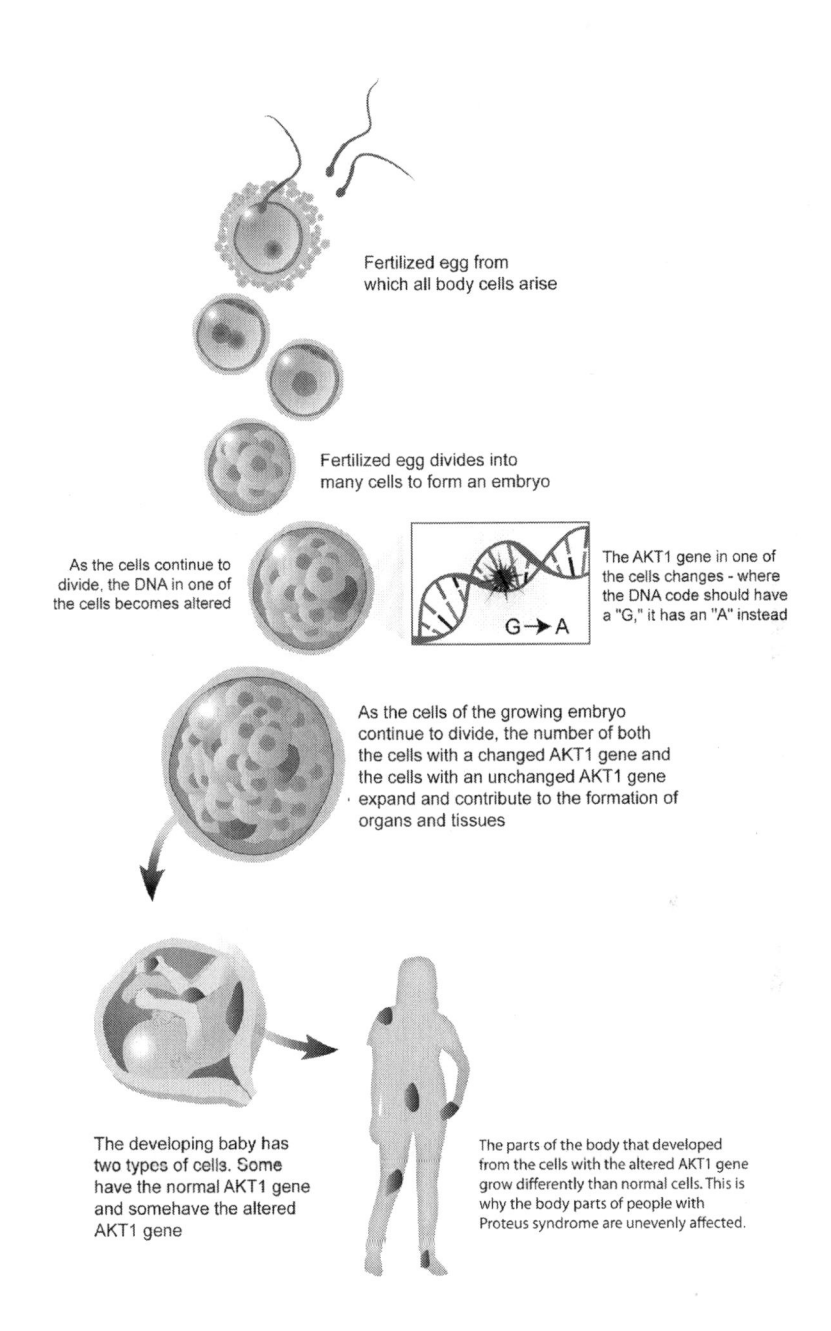

Mosaicism in Proteus Syndrome, National Institute of Health Human Genome Project

Besides overgrowth of limbs, Proteus syndrome also causes a variety of skin lesions and thickening of the soles of the feet. Some patients have neurological complications, such as mental retardation, seizures and vision loss. Blood vessel malformations are also associated with Proteus syndrome, and individuals with the condition are at greatly increased risk for deep vein thrombosis and pulmonary embolism.

Management of the Proteus syndrome requires a team of specialists with knowledge of the wide array of manifestations and complications of the disorder.

Courtesy: National Human Genome Research Institute.

FREQUENTLY ASKED QUESTIONS ABOUT PROTEUS SYNDROME
Answers provided by Dr. Leslie Biesecker

I have just found out that my child has Proteus Syndrome, what do I do first?
First, find a general doctor who you have a high confidence in, to act as advisor or case manager. This could be a paediatrician, GP or clinical geneticist. Orthopaedics should get involved early on to get acquainted with the child from an early age. Beyond that, the evaluations should be symptom driven.

Are there any annual checkups that I should look into?
Proteus Syndrome should be treated symptomatically and individually. Annual examinations are a very good idea and because the disorder is progressive, you will want to keep a track of it.

Can adults with PS have children?
There are no confirmed cases of PS where it has occurred twice in the same family. If the theory about PS is correct, we would

not expect this to happen very often, if at all. Because this disorder is rare, there are few patients to base this on. In the end, decisions about reproduction in people who have, or are at risk for a potentially inherited disorder, are personal and private.

I have a child with PS, will future children have it too?
There are no known instances in which an expert has confirmed the diagnosis of Proteus syndrome, with more than one person affected in the same family. The theory about Proteus syndrome suggests that this should be true. We advise families that the risk of recurrence is most likely the same as the risk for a family who does not have a person affected with Proteus syndrome, which is probably less than 1 in a million. We also believe that an adult with Proteus has the same low risk of having an affected child.

Although this appears to be true, it must be borne in mind that Proteus is a rare disorder, so no one has enough experience to be certain of these estimates. However, there is nothing to suggest they are incorrect.

Did I do something wrong in pregnancy?
There are no factors in common among mums who have had a child with Proteus that would suggest that something in pregnancy caused the baby to be affected. Also, the incidence of Proteus seems to be the same all over the world, and there are no prenatal factors that could cause such a rare disorder and be common to so many people around the world.

Is Proteus Syndrome life threatening?
This is unknown. From reading medical articles, it appears that there are many more affected children than adults, consistent with possible early mortality risks. Such estimates are frequently wrong as there are other potential explanations. However, there are a couple of factors that suggest the risk may be real. First, there are a number of patients with Proteus who have had tumours, and some of those have been serious. Second, there are

a number of persons with Proteus who have died from blood clots that started in the legs and then broke free and went to the lungs, causing death.

We do not know how often either of these happen, but it is possible that one of these may cause there to be fewer adults than children. For details on the issue of blood clots, please contact us regarding the article in the February 2000 edition of the U.S. Proteus syndrome foundation newsletter. In so far as the tumour issue is concerned, we do not have enough evidence that the risk is real, nor do we see a sufficiently consistent pattern of tumours to recommend specific screening. For the time being, regular medical checkups will have to suffice. We are well aware that "iffy" information like this is at best unsatisfactory, and at worst frightening and frustrating. We and others are working hard to gather information through clinical research studies to try to answer these questions in a more clear manner.

In discovering the cause of Proteus Syndrome, what kind of treatment will you be able to offer your patients? Will you be able to develop early detection of Proteus for prospective parents?

The discovery will definitely allow us to make the diagnosis earlier using molecular DNA testing. The identification of the mutated gene, and the fact that it is also mutated in some cancers, means that new drugs that are being developed for tumours with mutation in this same gene, may work on patients with Proteus syndrome. We are hoping to start a therapeutic trial in the near future.

Dr. Biesecker's research focuses on understanding the relationship of genomic variation to health and disease. Currently, his laboratory is engaged in studies in two main areas: classic genotype-phenotype studies of genetic disorders of development and growth, and new approaches to hypothesis generating clinical genomics research. The goals of his research program are to improve the medical care of patients affected by these disorders, provide generalised knowledge about the broad field of genetic disease and better understand basic mechanisms of normal and abnormal human development and physiology. His group studies several multiple anomalies syndromes, including Proteus syndrome. To further elucidate the clinical manifestations of these multiple anomaly syndromes, Dr. Biesecker's group takes advantage of the clinical resources available through the Mark O. Hatfield Clinical Research Centre on the main National Institute of Health campus, Bethesda, Maryland, USA.

In order to find the genes that are altered in these syndromes, Dr. Biesecker's group performs classical laboratory-based positional cloning studies, which determines genotype-phenotype correlations and uses animal models to investigate the pathogenetic mechanisms of these disorders. Protocols aimed at understanding the disorders listed above, as well as other disorders having manifestations that overlap with these disorders, are actively recruiting individuals for study. Many patients are invited for evaluation at the Clinical Research Centre, where they undergo extensive and sophisticated phenotypic assessments to generate data essential for understanding the range and variability of these rare disorders.

Dr. Biesecker can be reached for questions and concerns at the following:

(301) 402-2041
(301) 402-2170
leslieb@helix.nih.gov
Building 49, Room 4A56
9 Convent Dr, MSC 4472
Bethesda, MD 20892-4472, USA

DEATH OF "THE ELEPHANT MAN."

An inquest on the body of Joseph Merrick, better known as the "Elephant Man," was held yesterday at the London Hospital by Mr. Baxter. Charles Merrick, of Church-gate, Leicester, a hairdresser, identified the body as that of his nephew. The deceased was 29 years of age, and had followed no occupation. From birth he had been deformed, but he got much worse of late. He had been in the hospital four or five years. His parents were in no way afflicted, and the father, an engine driver, is alive now. Mr. Ashe, house surgeon, said he was called to the deceased at 3 30 p.m. on Friday, and found him dead. It was expected that he would die suddenly. There were no marks of violence, and the death was quite natural. The man had great overgrowth of the skin and bone, but he did not complain of anything. Witness believed that the exact cause of death was asphyxia, the back of his head being greatly deformed, and while the patient was taking a natural sleep the weight of the head overcame him, and so suffocated him. The coroner said that the man had been sent round the shows as a curiosity, and when death took place it was decided as a matter of prudence to hold this inquest. Mr. Hodges, another house surgeon, stated that on Friday last he went to visit the deceased, and found him lying across the bed dead. He was in a ward specially set apart for him. Witness did not touch him. Nurse Ireland, of the Blizzard Ward, said the deceased was in her charge. She saw him on Friday morning, when he appeared in his usual health. His midday meal was taken in to him, but he did not touch it. The coroner, in summing up, said there could be no doubt that death was quite in accordance with the theory put forward by the doctor. The jury accepted this view, and returned a verdict to the effect that death was due to suffocation from the weight of the head pressing on the windpipe.

Inquest into the death of Joseph Merrick.
The London Times 1990.

A computerised scientific, recreation of Joseph's face had he not developed Proteus Syndrome and possible NF1 (Neurofibromatosis 1), based on scans of his relatives on both the Potterton and Merrick sides.
(Discovery Health, "The Plight of the Elephant Man, 2002).

APPENDIX B

BEING A MOTHER OF A PROTEUS CHILD
AN ESSAY BY TRACEY WHITEWOOD-NEAL, MBE
of the Proteus Syndrome Foundation, UK

"I make my bread and butter from mothers like you who tell me there's something wrong with Johnny's little finger."

This remark was made by a doctor to a friend of mine whose son had Proteus Syndrome. The truth is that few doctors had ever heard of the condition before 1979. They knew nothing about it. It has taken a long time and much effort to convince doctors that, as parents, we need to know what we are dealing with here. In a way, it was a relief, finally to be given a name for our son Jordan's condition. However, getting the diagnosis of Proteus Syndrome (PS) was just the start of a new journey.

There appeared to be no information and no support groups. We felt lost and alone. We soon discovered, not only that PS was very rare, (only 120 cases had been reported world wide), but also that it was progressive in nature and very varied in its effects. The majority of sufferers were boys, and most PS children died young.

PS can cause abnormal and accelerated growth to any part of the body, most noticeably to the hands, legs and face. As time went by, doctors told us it was thought that Joseph Merrick, *The Elephant Man*, had suffered from PS. That in itself was quite a shock. Merrick, we knew, had died at twenty-seven. Proteus is relentless in its progression and, as the years went by we had to watch, as the disease took its toll on most parts of Jordan's body. Jordan has had to endure operations from the age of two weeks. These were mostly to try and stop his legs from growing crooked.

Countless surgeries failed to stop the excessive growth. This resulted in tremendous pain and the loss of the use of both legs. After a few years of contemplation and discussion, Jordan came to the conclusion that he would be better off without his legs. He had an above-knee amputation of his right leg in September 2009. The operation went reasonably smoothly, and Jordan pushed surgeons for a date for the other leg. This was done in February 2010. Jordan now uses prosthetic legs but has not looked back, and is confident he has made the right decision. The pain has gone and he can move around more easily.

But PS never sleeps. We have learnt never to take it for granted. Jordan had to undergo plastic surgery to reduce the size of the large, clumpy fingers on his left hand. He has had surgery for cancerous tumours. He has curvature of the spine. In 2011, he was found to have two clots in his lungs. This was alarming, as deep vein thrombosis and the resulting pulmonary embolism has claimed the lives of several PS children we know. Jordan has been treated for this, and will need to take blood thinners for the rest of his life.

When Jordan was just two, we found hope in discovering the Proteus Syndrome Foundation (PSF) on the Internet. This group in America had been running for a few years, had established a medical advisory board, and was working in partnership with a research project into the cause of the condition at the National Institute of Health in Washington. I decided to start a UK branch of the Proteus Syndrome Foundation. The work gives me a focus for my energies and I find it helpful to do something positive as a result of this major event in our lives

In April 2011, after 16 years of tireless research, the workers at the National Institute found the genetic cause of Proteus Syndrome! This is a wonderful breakthrough! They can now focus on developing a treatment for Proteus, to turn off the gene by drug therapy and stop it in its tracks! We have to believe in a better future for Jordan and all those like him.

So what advice can I give to parents of newly diagnosed children, or to those entering young adulthood, with a changing body image? Support is there. Please get connected. You can get in touch with us at www.proteus-syndrome.org.uk

If you are interested to read more about the research, turn to http://www.genome.gov/proteus

The other thing you should do is to keep up-to-date records of everything, so that doctors can more easily understand what is going on. And finally there is now, as there was not before, a real hope for the future for our bent, bruised and ultimately courageous children.

Many thanks to Richard and Colleen Baines (Australia)
for their support and input in writing this article.

APPENDIX C

PERSONAL ACCOUNTS

We interviewed three people who live with Proteus Syndrome in our time: Jordan Whitewood-Neal of England, Lisa Bartlett of Australia, and Brian Richards of the United States. These are their stories.

JORDON WHITEWOOD-NEAL

Jordan Whitewood-Neal (Tracey Whitewood-Neal, Proteus Syndrome Foundation, UK. Copyright 2012. All rights reserved).

Introduction by Jordan's mother, Tracey Whitewood-Neal, MBE:

At our 2008 Family weekend, Jordan asked if he could say a few words. Jordan, on his own, wrote the speech below. He received a standing ovation and quite a few tears, especially from me, his proud mum. I hope you too find this inspirational.

Jordan speaks on his feelings about Proteus Syndrome:

"Ladies and gentlemen I believe you all know me, but for those who don't, I'm Jordan Whitewood-Neal and I'm kind of new to this, so you'll have to bear with me. I'm not here to tell a story or to give advice, but to give some sort of direction.

So, as you all know, Proteus is an overgrowth syndrome, which causes bone, organs and tissue to grow out of control. For some Proteus sufferers it is a problem, a wall on the road to the future, but for me, and hopefully many more, it has become a way of life, and everything is considered no different from the way anyone else lives.

Through my long 13 years, I have come across many hurdles. Some have been big, some small, but I can tell you this, every one of those hurdles I have conquered. I've wheeled my manual wheelchair in a mini-marathon of 2.5 kilometres, I've walked when the doctors have said I couldn't, I've run when the doctors have said it's impossible, and I've played football when the doctors have said my legs just wouldn't take it. I defied everything they said and I went further: I played golf, basketball, I swam and what ever I wanted to do, I did it. So as I said, I play golf and it's keeping me energetic and fit and I find it fun.

Proteus to me has never ever got in the way of my education. I'm top in most of my classes and hopefully will be taking three GCSE's early, which are end-of-year eleven tests in English, art, and possibly L.C.T. I'm also now in year nine and am going to become a peer mentor to a selected student, which I believe will be good for both me and the student I mentor, especially if they are being bullied, because I have experienced it myself. Some of you might know this already but when I finish school I want to go to college, then university to study to be an architect. Now I dream and when I reach that dream, I've won. I might not have won every battle but I will definitely be able to say that I won the war.

Proteus Syndrome does not only affect the sufferer but also the family, some closer, some wider. Sometimes it affects the mum, dad, brother or sister, but then sometimes it can affect cousins, uncles, aunties and grandparents as well. Whatever happens, you must never ever let Proteus split up those close to you, never give in, always keep going and keep your mind strong—which leads me into a little story.

Two boys once came up to me and very politely said "Excuse me, do you mind telling us what you have?" That was the breakthrough. I told them what I have and they were really nice. They are the people that I have loads of respect for. It made me realise that having Proteus is not a curse, it's just the way we are. We should not be judged on the shape of our body but what's up here in our heads and what we fill it with. That's how I want people to think.

Now, I'd like to unfortunately turn to the sometimes hard difficulties that Proteus brings me, and these problems probably occur in many others. At least once in our childhood or maybe even past that stage, all of us who suffer Proteus will be stared at, bullied and sometimes just go through a stage where we feel angry at everything and spend our time just wondering why me, why not anyone else. I would know--I've been through the stage myself. But luckily there'll be a stage where you feel absolutely fantastic, you'll feel energetic, you'll feel happy, and you won't even care if you have Proteus. That feeling would continue for how ever long you want, and I'm currently going through that phase.

I want to really focus on school, I want to go out with friends downtown and just hang around like any old teenager should. I want to play golf, listen to music and just have a good time no matter what I have.

And the happiest thing I can say is that, sometimes I completely forget that I have Proteus, even though subconsciously, I know I do. But to tell the truth, who really cares? That is the message I want to get across: that nothing should hold us back, nothing should stop us from doing what we want, and nothing's ever easy, but what's the fun in something if it's not a challenge?

So thank you for listening. I hope that everything I said gave each and every one of you some help and that you really believed in what I said."

Jordan Whitewood-Neal

Lisa Bartlett. Copyright 2012.
All rights reserved.

LISA BARTLETT

Lisa hails from Melbourne, Australia. She and her husband Ian have a daughter, Natalie, and a son, Daniel. Neither of them has Proteus Syndrome.

Lisa writes:
"I was born with varicose veins and a cafe spot on my arms. My parents were told it was nothing. There were no other signs. Every doctor my mum took me to, said there was nothing wrong. When I started to crawl, I broke three fingers and a thumb. They grew back, bent. When mum took me to the doctors, on the day I broke them, they decided there may be something wrong and I was sent to a specialist. That doctor said I had Neurofibromatosis. It wasn't until I was twenty one, that I was told I had Proteus Syndrome. Over time, I developed curvature of the spine, a lump on my head and I have had a few operations.

I went to regular school, as there is nothing wrong with my brain. I am the least affected in the world and hardly anyone notices there is anything wrong. I don't let anything get in my way and don't find it a big deal. Sure, there are things I can't do, like stand for long periods of time or lift heavy things, but my family never let me get away with anything, and I was not allowed to use my disease as an excuse. I was brought up to believe I was as good as anybody else. My parents and four brothers were the best. I am married with two children. My daughter is seventeen and my son is fifteen. They haven't got Proteus, thank God.

No matter what happens in life, you have to believe you are worth it and that you have every right to be here. I have my family to thank and besides, there are heaps worse that could happen.

So my question for you all is: What would you do if you were having a child and were told they were going to have Proteus Syndrome? Would you have the child or not? Remember that not everyone gets it the same. I'm the least affected, whereas Joseph Merrick had the worst form. Let's say the doctors cannot tell you how badly affected your child will be. It's a hard one to answer, I know. I asked my mum this same question when I was six. She said that she wanted a little girl so much and that she was so blessed to have such a special one.

When I was growing, they didn't know as much about Proteus as they know now. They said I had a fifty percent chance of passing it on. I wouldn't have any test at all, because I wouldn't want to know. I'd hope for the best and deal with it, if it happened. That would be hard for me, because I would feel like I was to blame, for all the pain the child had ahead of them.

When I heard they found the cause of Proteus, I wasn't sure how I felt. It's good, of course, in so many ways. But it's also a bit of a downer, because from what I understand, there's more chance of getting cancer, as if there isn't enough to deal with. I hope they can help the little ones though."

Lisa Bartlett

BRIAN RICHARDS

Brian Richards. Copyright 2012. All rights reserved

Brian Richards is from Charleston, South Carolina. He graduated from Delaware State University with a Bachelor's in Social Work. Currently, he lives in Delaware, where he works as a counsellor and mentor to youths with disabilities. Brian was featured in the Discovery Channel TV documentary, "Meet the *Elephant Man*" which first aired in March 2011. He is an accomplished artist of scroll saw works, an intricate form of woodworking, that can take months to complete.

"My Experiences as a Proteus Man:
A Uniquely Perfect and Rare Breed

Introduction
My name is Brian, I am 27 years old and I have Proteus Syndrome, which is a rare genetic disorder. I am writing this to shed some light on how Proteus Syndrome patients live and to show what we have to endure in our daily lives. Proteus Syndrome is a disease which leads to many anomalies which have affected my appearance and my ability to do many things

that "normal" people can do. To date, I have had 36 surgeries to correct some of these problems and to help me be as active as I can be. Proteus Syndrome is an unexpected visitor in your life, as it is not passed down genetically but occurs after conception, when a mutation occurs and spreads to different areas of the developing embryo. I am lucky because I have a mild case of Proteus Syndrome, but it affects me from head to toe. My feet have always been a problem. I had gigantism with some of my toes, which led to amputation of four of them. I have large bony tumours, called osteomas, on the bottoms of both feet, which cannot be surgically removed due to the unusual skin, called rugae, which looks like brain tissue. Because of the toe amputations and bony tumours on the bottoms of my feet, I have to wear specially made orthotics at all times and wear the biggest, widest shoes possible.

Bony tumours, or osteomas, crop up in various places and I have had them surgically removed from over my eyes, in my ears and even from my fingers. The problem with this type of surgery is the osteomas have a way of growing back, sometimes worse than they were previously. As a result, I have developed deafness in one ear and now have to wear a hearing aid. When I had surgery done on several fingers to straighten them, the bones grew back faster and some of my fingers became frozen, so I cannot make a fist or bend the fingers. Handwriting has been difficult and ever since grade school, I have had to use a computer to write instead of pen or pencil. My knees are also victims of bony overgrowths and I have had numerous surgeries to remove bone, and even an extra kneecap. As a result, walking long distances or running is out of the question due to the pain from overuse.

Internally, Proteus Syndrome can lead to various problems, too. I was diagnosed with having seizures, which were the result of a venous malformation in my brain. Fortunately, I had a great surgeon, who successfully removed this malformation, and I have been seizure free-ever since. In my late teens, it was discovered that I had cysts in my lungs, a condition called "bullous emphysema." I have to be careful to avoid exposure to chemicals or other things which may further damage my lungs.

I also have to be careful to avoid respiratory infections as they will be difficult to treat and coughing could lead to my lung collapsing from the stress. My liver has also been affected, due to a problem with the blood flow -- another side effect of Proteus.

Because of the asymmetrical bone growth, my spine has been badly affected. The vertebrae in my neck have fused so my head tilts to one side and limits my ability to look around or move to a more comfortable position. As I have grown, the scoliosis and curvature of my neck and upper spine are starting to impinge on my spinal cord and oesophagus. I have vertebrae which have started growing inward toward the spine. This affects the type and amount of food I can eat, since I have more difficulty swallowing. I have been cautioned to monitor some of my more strenuous activities as any damage to my upper neck can affect my spinal cord, possibly leading to paralysis. Sleeping can be difficult, because of general discomfort while lying down, from the inability to freely move my neck and from joint pain. Fatty tumours, or lipomas, are benign tumours that also grow in various spots and can be uncontrollable with surgery when they return. I have them between my toes and in my abdomen. It was the second occurrence of lipomas at age 3 which led my surgeon to suspect that I probably had a genetic disorder.

Life with Proteus Syndrome is challenging, but it is who I am. Whenever I go for another check-up, I am not surprised to learn about new problems. I used to think once I reached adulthood, that things would level off, but the doctors are finding medical problems that can still occur. Deep vein blood clots (thromboses) are an everyday concern, as it is one of the leading causes of death for Proteus Syndrome patients. I have learned that being conservative in many of my treatments is the way to go, as sometimes more is not better. I have learned various ways to manage my pain, such as using meditation, acupuncture, or alternative medicines.

But I also enjoy my life -- I do as much as I can and try to use my talents to be productive. It amazes me that only a handful of doctors know about Proteus Syndrome. I am tired of them not understanding it. People who don't understand Proteus Syndrome often stop and stare, which is a bit unnerving at times.

Life with Proteus Syndrome and the hardships
Surgery is very common for a person with Proteus Syndrome. Things that seem easy or routine with normal people are difficult with us because our bodies are constructed differently. Differences include a general asymmetry of the bones, the fusion of the neck and back vertebrae, contortion of organs caused by misshaped skeletal features. Complications are one of the hardest things to overcome with Proteus Syndrome. When performing a surgery on a Proteus patient, sometimes the less you do is better. People with Proteus can regenerate bone or fatty tissue. If a doctor does a surgery and cuts into any bone, then that bone can start regenerating, forming bony overgrowths. This causes more pain for the Proteus patient. We also get bone spurs that start to form at the site where the surgery was performed. I had surgery on my hand to straighten crooked fingers when I was about 9 or 10. The doctor cut a pie-shaped wedge from my finger and put screws in to hold the bones in place while it healed. When I returned to him to get the screws removed, the bone had already grown over the screws. The doctor gave me no pain medication because it was supposedly a simple procedure. As he turned the screws, it caused great pain and agony. I remember that incident well and today it still haunts me. This brings me to my next topic, Post Traumatic Stress Disorder or PTSD.

PTSD is a disorder used to describe a severe and ongoing emotional reaction that results from exposure to extreme stress and/or trauma. Clinically, such events involve actual or threatened death, serious physical injury, or a threat to physical and/or psychological well-being, to a degree that usual psychological defences are incapable of coping with. It might cause things like nightmares, flashbacks, emotional detachment or numbing of feelings, insomnia, avoidance of reminders and extreme distress. People normally associate PTSD with military veterans and people who have been victims of abuse. I am living proof that too many surgeries as a child can lead to PTSD.

Bullying is an unfortunate part of growing up with Proteus Syndrome. I remember getting picked on, mostly by older kids and adults. I recently read some of the diaries that I wrote a long time ago and it took me by surprise. I remember some of the torment, but not all of it. I read in my diary about kids calling me Frankenstein, a mutant, retarded, and many other names. Some asked me if I ever washed my neck because of the brown café au lait spot or hyper-pigmentation on my neck. I remember getting picked last for most sports. I wish kids and adults would understand that just because people are different does not mean they are bad. One Proteus kid told me, "one teacher at my school said that God cursed me because of something I did in this life or a past life. That is why I am so deformed." That was absolutely devastating for this kid. For someone to tell you that is just plain wrong.

Relationships are very difficult for kids with disabilities, and many young people with Proteus Syndrome suffer from low self-esteem. Everyone wants to be attracted to his or her significant other. Unfortunately, some people with Proteus think because they are different, no one will find them attractive. Even reassurance does not help. I remember girls saying to me, "Brian, you look good", and my reply was "What are you smoking, because I might need some?" It was a joke to me because all the torment I received during my years of growing up made me bury my head in shame.

I remember a girl I liked in kindergarten. We became boyfriend and girlfriend and liked each other until the second grade. Then she told me something that affected me for many years. She broke up with me for my best friend. She told me she did it because she wanted someone 'normal'. To a kid, that is devastating. I then began to believe that because I was not "society-normal," no girl would ever love me. Fortunately, I have met a wonderful woman and we have a serious and loving relationship. There remains hope for all.

I have spoken with a few children and young adults with Proteus and they find relationships hard too. I talk to one individual monthly and most of the time it is about relationships that he is going through. He would say, "She broke up with me for my friend. How could my friend do that to me?" Or, "This girl cheated on me and just played me." Sometimes he would say, "She liked me, but not anymore. Why?" For many people, relationships are hard and you have to continually work on them. Some, on the other hand, just do not get that chance.

The other problem that I see in relationships is that we never know how long they will last. People say, "You can be dead today or in a hundred years". That is very true, but for us it is a little different. People with Proteus can die suddenly and for many different reasons. It is a little scary to think about this, especially while in a relationship. Don't get me wrong, people living with Proteus can live very long and reasonably healthy lives. Some are less fortunate and have short lives. It depends on the extent of their disease. Fortunately, I have a relatively mild case of Proteus Syndrome. People are uncomfortable with the uncertainty that something life threatening could crop up at any time.

Goals
One thing I have noticed about children and adults with Proteus is that no matter what happens, we do not give up. I know a kid

that cannot pedal a bike with his feet, so his wonderful mother got him a bike that has the pedals on the handlebars. This way he can feel a bit more normal and enjoy something that is taken for granted by so many people. People think just because we are different we cannot do many things. That is so wrong. Children are very adaptable and Proteus children even more so. We always strive for the best. If there is a way of doing something and a person with Proteus wants to do it, then it gets done. It might not be the most conventional way of doing it, but it still allows us that chance. I tell kids with and without Proteus that you never give up. If there is a way, you must find it. Never give up on your hopes and dreams.

For example, I have always loved the martial arts. My parents always said I would hurt myself, because of my hands, feet or bad knee. My doctors agreed. So what do I do? I train every day at one of the world's hardest marital arts (in my opinion) Northern Shaolin Kung Fu. When parents or doctors say that I cannot do something, I feel as if they have given up on me before I have even tried. That inspires me even more to try. You learn from your experiences in life, and of course you might get hurt or mess something up, but that is a part of learning.

One thing I know for certain, no kid with Proteus will ever be considered a quitter. These kids try so hard in everything they do that it would put others to shame. People look at me and say, "you have been through so much, how do you keep moving on?" I tell them that I don't ever quit--I just take one step at a time. A kid with Proteus will tell you the same thing. Sometimes it is frustrating or makes you sad, but we just move on. For many years, as I lifted weights, I looked at these kids for inspiration. They inspire me more than anything in this world. I just look at their pictures while training and even put some pictures of them on my wall. People asked me what all the kid's pictures were about. I told them, "They are my inspiration." I give these kids the credit for my success, because without them, I might have given up. Since they do not give up, neither do I.

Adaptations
There are two different forms of adaptation with Proteus Syndrome. One form is adaptation of the body; the other is of the mind. People with Proteus have a different body structure where asymmetry is common, including gigantism of fingers or toes, facial features, leg or arm lengths, etc. As malformations surge during early growth, the body of the Proteus patient adapts in various ways to accommodate the malformations. Most Proteus patients have different feet. They might have gigantic toes, as I did, needing to have them amputated as I did. I also have bones on the arch of my feet that project downward and do not allow me to walk without special insoles in my shoes.

Other bony malformations are common. I have five curves in my spine and neck, but fortunately for me, all of those curves balance each other out. I walk straight, and can sit upright, all because my body has adjusted to the asymmetry. The soles of the feet of Proteus patients have highly abnormal folds of skin that easily become infected and lead to painful walking. Interventions are often needed to facilitate walking for those people with Proteus who are lucky enough to walk.

Adaptation of the mind is conditioning oneself to accept what he or she has and how to deal with it. With Proteus Syndrome, I have had to adapt to many things such as writing, driving, swimming, walking, running, martial arts, cleaning, and tolerating pain. When you look at a Proteus patient, you see various deformities. With such deformities, I've had to learn how to accept my limitations and how to participate in activities. In many of my kung fu classes, I have learned to accept what I can't change and focus on what I can do.

Because our body structure is different, Proteus patients have to find different ways to do things. For instance, I hold a pool cue differently, because of the enlargement of one of my fingers. I still play pool, and I am very good at this sport, but others can't shoot like me, because of how I hold my hand. Sometimes being different has its advantages and other times great disadvantages. When it comes to the disadvantages just remember one thing, at least you can still do it. Even though it might be hard or painful to do something, we find a way to succeed.

Personal Accomplishments
Survival is one of the hardest parts of Proteus. What I mean by survival is not like living on a desert island, but instead surviving everyday things like school, family, and kids antagonising you, people always asking your parents, "What's wrong with your kid?", etc. Survival is just one part of life. You learn to love yourself, despite your imperfections.

I tell a lot of my teen patients that I once had an anger problem. They look at me funny because now I have calmed down and have no anger issues now. To me the anger came from many things. The first was that kids never understood what I was going through. They pointed, stared, and mocked me. I showed the anger first to make the bullies go away. I was also angry because I hated having Proteus. I was so upset because I could not have a normal life. I thought I was ugly. On my 16th birthday, coming home from a doctor's appointment with my mother, I started to break down and cry. It was because I had bottled up my hatred for myself and for others so long, I could not take it anymore. Since that day, I have never cried again. Not for funerals, operations, or pain. I came to realise that I was different but God loved me no matter what. My parents loved me as well. Most of all, I should love myself. That day I finally accepted what I was. A man. I saw past the surgeries, scars, and the disease. I saw the man I had become.

Another reason for my anger was my past. I am happy to say that I could not have asked for better parents. They looked out for my best interests, even if that meant I would not like the outcome. All my surgeries were based around Christmas break, Easter break, or my summer vacation. When looking back, that is all I saw. It was a past of just surgeries. No fun. Finally, I was angry because some doctors treated me as a guinea pig. I felt that a lot of my care was just experimentation. Some doctors would poke while others would prod. Doctors frequently had no answers about my condition or treatment. However, that has improved over time, as more information is collected about Proteus Syndrome.

Fortunately, I grew up and realised that I was not as bad off as some, and that everyone lives through some hard times. I believe these reasons have led me to be the man I am today.

Grade School was the hardest time for me because kids never knew what was going on with me. They would point, stare, and call me very hurtful names. "Children", as I like to say, "do not have censors." What I mean by that is if kids want to know something, they will ask with no hesitation. To them it is not hurtful, because all they are looking for is the truth, and as many people say, "knowledge is power." I remember in second grade I had to walk around each day during lunchtime with an intravenous line that administered antibiotics for a brain infection. I wore it for six months. Kids made fun of it, but I had to have it.

Boy Scouts helped me tremendously. They showed me that just because I was different, I would not be treated differently. They had to exempt me from some merit badges because I could not swim, but for the most part, I did everything. I learned about camping, wilderness survival, rifle and shotgun shooting, and how to use a bow and arrow. I remember trying to use the bow and arrow after just having hand surgery. I had screws through my finger, but I never gave up hope. I finally became an Eagle

Scout at the age of 17. I could have received it earlier, but I moved to Delaware, and that pushed me back a little. I had 27 merit badges, six more than needed, and I had many more awards. Being in leadership might have helped me with my next topic, which is something that I truly love.

Martial arts are a big part of my life. I was always told that I would never be able to do them, even though it was my dream to learn. I pushed away all the stereotypes and began kickboxing. I later studied Muay Thai, and then my passion in martial arts came. I entered Northern Shaolin Kung Fu. I learned how to make myself strong, how to heal others, how to meditate, use my chi, and most of all, how to accept my differences and use them to my advantages. I was inducted into the Martial Arts Hall of Fame in 2010. I pushed myself harder than any other student. Martial arts are my way of life now. I use my martial arts for myself. I do not have to look at another person and say, "Boy, I could never do that". It is not about them, but about self-improvement. People, especially those with a disease, compare themselves to others. Marital arts prove you don't have to. The only person to impress is yourself and you have to look back to when you first started and see how much progress you made.

Skydiving is another achievement I'm proud of. Many people told me that I was crazy for doing this. They said, "It would hurt your body and lungs". I did what they called the hardcore jump, which is just higher than the normal jump. I loved it and proved people wrong. Skydiving was another dream I wanted to experience and ultimately achieved. This just shows you that nothing is impossible if you have willpower

College was a great time in my life. Even though I tell people I hate school, I learned a lot and needed the experience. College showed me that, though kids can be cruel when they are younger, they do act more mature when they get older. I had no problems at college. I went everyday and never skipped class. The students there called me "The Professor". That is because I always asked questions, and sometimes I had the answers when the professors didn't. I learned that, even though my early days in school had been tough, college life was much more tolerable. People showed me that it is not what is on the outside, but rather, what is inside. I feel that all people should be able to have the college experience. I received my Bachelor's Degree in Social Work and have counselled young and old alike. Perhaps my experiences with Proteus Syndrome have been to some advantage. I also enjoy woodworking and am extremely proficient in scroll saw art. I have manufactured hundreds of intricately cut items, which I list on Facebook to supplement my income.

Considering my hand and finger problems, it amazes me how I can achieve such tedious tasks. Joseph Merrick, the so-called Elephant Man, also had Proteus Syndrome, but managed to construct models of buildings out of cardboard and even learned basket weaving. So my advice to people who are disabled is try to work. Try to do your best. Don't give up on yourself. Fight, just fight."

Brian Richards

APPENDIX D

BUILDING JOSEPH'S CATHEDRAL - TODAY!

Reverend Thomas Clay,
website author and master model builder.
(Rev. Thomas Clay. Copyright 2012.
All rights reserved).

The Rev. Thomas Davies Clay was ordained an Episcopal Priest in 1963. After serving as Rector of five southeastern churches for thirty years, he retired in 1998. From 2002 until 2007 he was a docent at the Washington National Cathedral. During this time he and his wife decided that they would like to visit European cathedrals. Thus began what will soon be a nine year *"cathedral quest"*, visiting over 165 European churches and cathedrals thus far.

In the early 90's, Thomas built two paper church models – Mont San Michel and Chartres Cathedral, not ever expecting to visit them. On their visit to France in 2005, to see these two churches plus a number of other French Gothic Cathedrals, he found a shop that sold other paper models. Thus began an interesting hobby of building paper models of churches that he has visited. Even more exciting is building models of churches that he will visit on the next cathedral quest.

By spending fifteen to twenty-five hours on each model, he becomes intimately familiar with all the architectural details. This makes visiting the real cathedral even more exciting. His paper models, which now number over 45, also include castles, palaces and important public buildings that he has visited. He presently owns more than 50 additional kits of places that he has visited. These models are bought from dealers all over the world. Thomas spends many hours searching web pages for new models.

In 2010 he designed a webpage - www.cathedralquest.com, which Mae Stroshane discovered, whilst researching more about Joseph's cathedral. Thomas confirmed that it is a model of Mainz Cathedral. He had recently purchased a reprinted kit of the same model from a dealer in Poland. The model was first published in the 1880s and republished in 1998. It took Thomas seventeen hours to construct his model. There are 127 parts, including many very small pinnacles. These are a challenge to a model maker with two hands. It would seem almost impossible for someone with the use of only one hand!

Thomas Clay:
"Joseph Merrick must have possessed exceptional skills to have made it. There were only 10 major sections - since the cathedral is symmetrical - the identical parts on each side had the same number, like both of the west towers were marked # 7 with all the components being numbered 7a, 7b, etc. Modern kits have a lot more numbers with indications where parts fit together. This model had none of that. It definitely is not a model for first time builders which makes Joseph's model even more remarkable. The directions were very brief and not very helpful so I had to spend a lot of time looking at the cover photo.

The following illustrations demonstrate the process of building this model, which is identical to Joseph's.

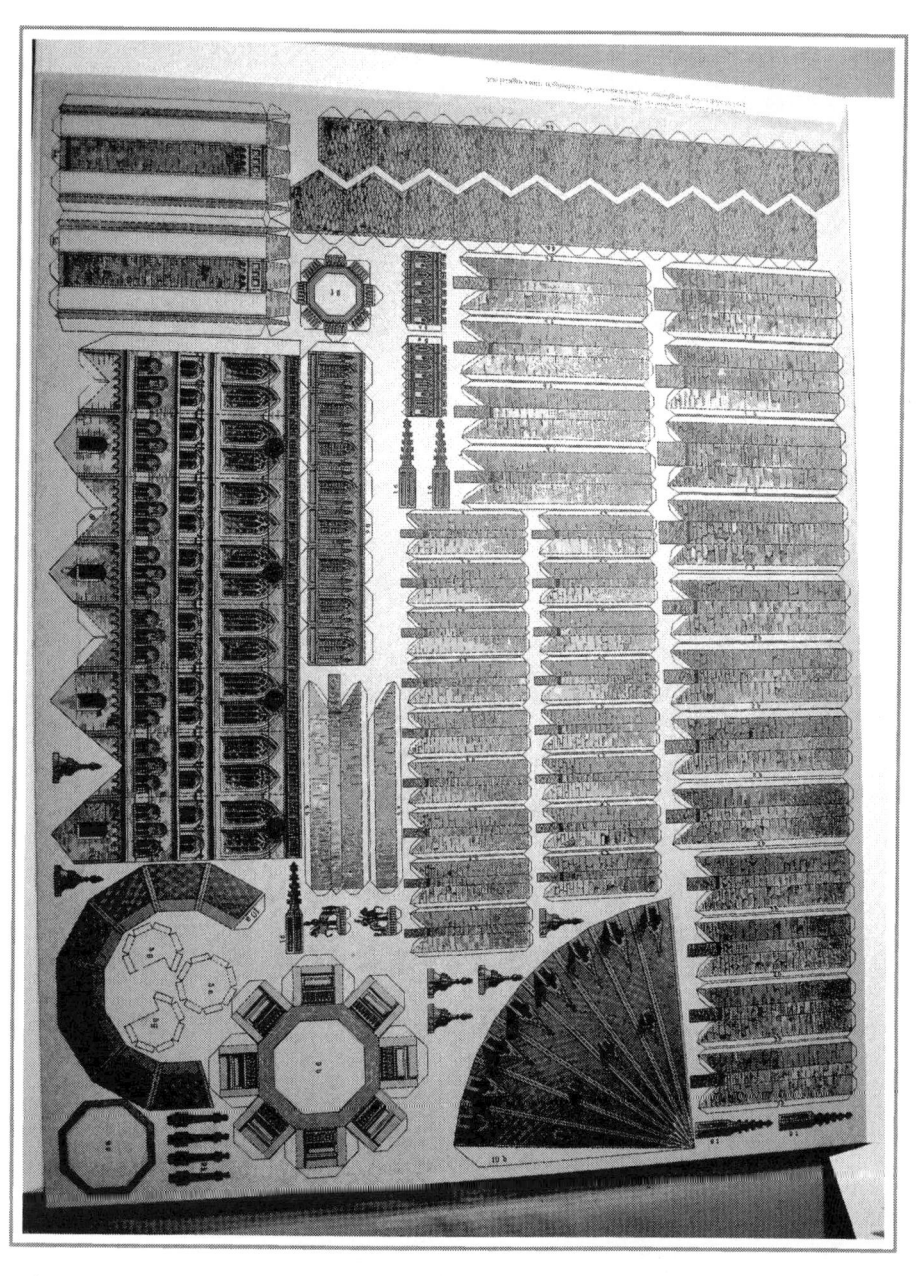

The exact same kit that Joseph built. Mainz Cathedral.
(Rev. Thomas Clay. Copyright 2012. All rights reserved).

Reverend Thomas Clay, building Joseph's church today. (Rev. Thomas Clay. Copyright 2012. All rights reserved).

147

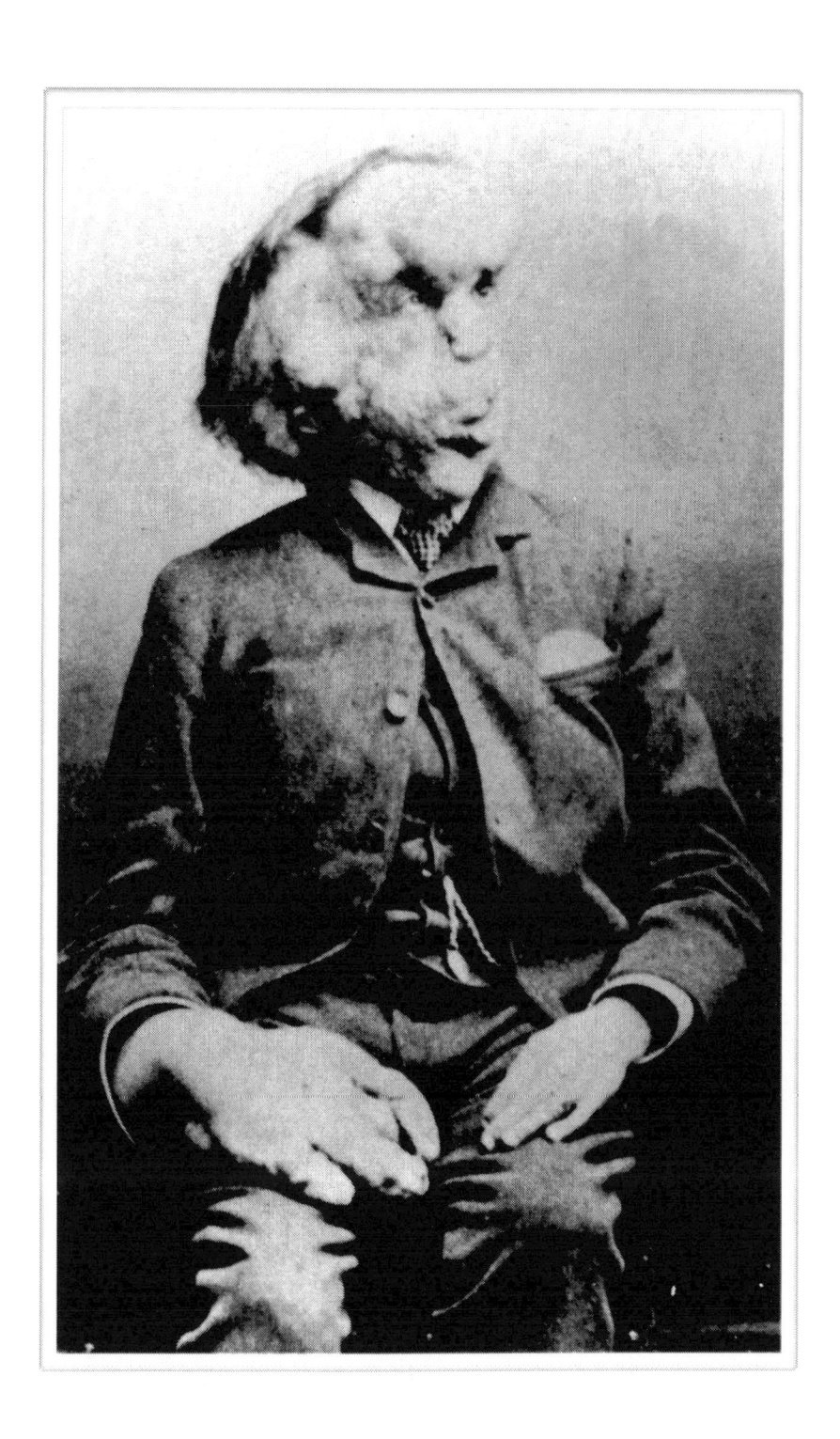

PREVIOUS PHOTO:
Joseph Merrick poses in his Sunday Best suit for a visiting card, circa 1889. He gave one of these to his spiritual counsellor, Reverend Tristram Valentine, and it was then passed on to a doctor's family before being returned to the London Hospital. It is the only known photograph of Joseph seated and fully dressed. (Royal London Hospital Museum Archives)

APPENDIX E

THE ELEPHANT MAN AND OTHER REMINISCENCES
By Frederick Treves

"In the Mile End Road, opposite to the London Hospital, there was (and possibly still is) a line of small shops. Among them was a vacant greengrocer's which was to let. The whole of the front of the shop, with the exception of the door, was hidden by a hanging sheet of canvas on which was the announcement that *The Elephant Man* was to be seen within and that the price of admission was two pence. Painted on the canvas in primitive colours was a life-size portrait of the Elephant Man. This very crude production depicted a frightful creature that could only have been possible in a nightmare. It was the figure of a man with the characteristics of an elephant.

The transfiguration was not far advanced. There was still more of the man than of the beast. This fact — that it was still human — was the most repellent attribute of the creature. There was nothing about it of the pitiableness of the misshapen or the deformed, nothing of the grotesqueness of the freak, but merely the loathsome insinuation of a man being changed into an animal. Some palm trees in the background of the picture suggested a jungle and might have led the imaginative to assume that it was in this wild that the perverted object had roamed.

When I first became aware of this phenomenon the exhibition was closed, but a well-informed boy sought the proprietor in a public house and I was granted a private view on payment of a shilling. The shop was empty and grey with dust. Some old tins and a few shrivelled potatoes occupied a shelf and some vague vegetable refuse the window. The light in the place was dim, being obscured by the painted placard outside.

The far end of the shop — where I expect the late proprietor sat at a desk — was cut off by a curtain or rather by a red tablecloth suspended from a cord by a few rings. The room was cold and dank, for it was the month of November. The year, I might say, was 1884.

The showman pulled back the curtain and revealed a bent figure crouching on a stool and covered by a brown blanket. In front of it, on tripod, was a large brick heated by a Bunsen burner. Over this the creature was huddled to warm itself. It never moved when the curtain was drawn back.

Locked up in an empty shop and lit by the faint blue light of the gas jet, this hunched-up figure was the embodiment of loneliness. It might have been a captive in a cavern or a wizard watching for unholy manifestations in the ghostly flame. Outside the sun was shining and one could hear the footsteps of the passers-by, a tune whistled by a boy and the companionable hum of traffic in the road.

The showman — speaking as if to a dog — called out harshly: "Stand up!" The thing arose slowly and let the blanket that covered its head and back fall to the ground. There stood revealed the most disgusting specimen of humanity that I have ever seen. In the course of my profession I had come upon lamentable deformities of the face due to injury or disease, as well as mutilations and contortions of the body depending upon like causes; but at no time had I met with such a degraded or perverted version of a human being as this lone figure displayed. He was naked to the waist, his feet were bare, he wore a pair of threadbare trousers that had once belonged to some fat gentleman's dress suit.

From the intensified painting in the street I had imagined *The Elephant Man* to be of gigantic size. This, however, was a little man below the average height and made to look shorter by the bowing of his back. The most striking feature about him was his enormous and misshapen head.

From the brow there projected a huge bony mass like a loaf, while from the back of the head hung a bag of spongy, fungous-looking skin, the surface of which was comparable to brown cauliflower. On the top of the skull were a few long lank hairs. The osseous growth on the forehead almost occluded one eye. The circumference of the head was no less than that of the man's waist.

From the upper jaw there projected another mass of bone. It protruded from the mouth like a pink stump, turning the upper lip inside out and making of the mouth a mere slobbering aperture. This growth from the jaw had been so exaggerated in the painting as to appear to be a rudimentary trunk or tusk. The nose was merely a lump of flesh, only recognisable as a nose from its position. The face was no more capable of expression than a block of gnarled wood. The back was horrible, because from it hung, as far down as the middle of the thigh, huge, sack-like masses of flesh covered by the same loathsome cauliflower skin.

The right arm was of enormous size and shapeless. It suggested the limb of the subject of elephantiasis. It was overgrown also with pendent masses of the same cauliflower-like skin. The hand was large and clumsy — a fin or paddle rather than a hand. There was no distinction between the palm and the back. The thumb had the appearance of a radish, while the fingers might have been thick, tuberous roots. As a limb it was almost useless. The other arm was remarkable by contrast. It was not only normal but was, moreover, a delicately shaped limb covered with fine skin and provided with a beautiful hand which any woman might have envied. From the chest hung a bag of the same repulsive flesh. It was like a dewlap suspended from the neck of a lizard. The lower limbs had the characters of the deformed arm. They were unwieldy, dropsical looking and grossly misshapen.

To add a further burden to his trouble the wretched man, when a boy, developed hip disease, which had left him permanently lame, so that he could only walk with a stick. He was thus denied all means of escape from his tormentors. As he told me later, he could never run away.

One other feature must be mentioned to emphasise his isolation from his kind. Although he was already repellent enough, there arose from the fungous skin-growth with which he was almost covered a very sickening stench which was hard to tolerate.

From the showman I learnt nothing about *The Elephant Man*, except that he was English, that his name was John Merrick and that he was twenty-one years of age. As at the time of my discovery of *The Elephant Man* I was the Lecturer on Anatomy at the Medical College opposite, I was anxious to examine him in detail and to prepare an account of his abnormalities.

I therefore arranged with the showman that I should interview his strange exhibit in my room at the college. I became at once conscious of a difficulty. *The Elephant Man* could not show himself in the streets. He would have been mobbed by the crowd and seized by the police. He was, in fact, as secluded from the world as the Man with the Iron Mask.

He had, however, a disguise, although it was almost as startling as he was himself. It consisted of a long black cloak which reached to the ground. Whence the cloak had been obtained I cannot imagine. I had only seen such a garment on the stage wrapped about the figure of a Venetian bravo.

The recluse was provided with a pair of bag-like slippers in which to hide his deformed feet. On his head was a cap of a kind that never before was seen. It was black like the cloak, had a wide peak, and the general outline of a yachting cap.

As the circumference of Merrick's head was that of a man's waist, the size of this headgear may be imagined. From the attachment of the peak a grey flannel curtain hung in front of the face. In this mask was cut a wide horizontal slit through which the wearer could look out. This costume, worn by a bent man hobbling along with a stick, is probably the most remarkable and the most uncanny that has as yet been designed. I arranged that Merrick should cross the road in a cab, and to insure his immediate admission to the college I gave him my card. This card was destined to play a critical part in Merrick's life.

I made a careful examination of my visitor, the result of which I embodied in a paper. I made little of the man himself. He was shy, confused, not a little frightened and evidently much cowed. Moreover, his speech was almost unintelligible. The great bony mass that projected from his mouth blurred his utterance and made the articulation of certain words impossible. He returned in a cab to the place of exhibition, and I assumed that I had seen the last of him, especially as I found next day that the show had been forbidden by the police and that the shop was empty.

I supposed that Merrick was imbecile and had been imbecile from birth. The fact that his face was incapable of expression, that his speech was a mere spluttering and his attitude that of one whose mind was void of all emotions and concerns gave grounds for this belief. The conviction was no doubt encouraged by the hope that his intellect was the blank I imagined it to be. That he could appreciate his position was unthinkable.

Here was a man in the heyday of youth who was so vilely deformed that everyone he met confronted him with a look of horror and disgust. He was taken about the country to be exhibited as a monstrosity and an object of loathing. He was shunned like a leper, housed like a wild beast, and got his only

153

view of the world from a peephole in a showman's cart. He was, moreover, lame, had but one available arm, and could hardly make his utterances understood. It was not until I came to know that Merrick was highly intelligent, that he possessed an acute sensibility and — worse than all — a romantic imagination that I realised the overwhelming tragedy of his life.

The episode of *The Elephant Man* was, I imagined, closed; but I was fated to meet him again — two years later — under more dramatic conditions. In England the showman and Merrick had been moved on from place to place by the police, who considered the exhibition degrading and among the things that could not be allowed. It was hoped that in the uncritical retreats of Mile End a more abiding peace would be found. But it was not to be. The official mind there, as elsewhere, very properly decreed that the public exposure of Merrick and his deformities transgressed the limits of decency. The show must close. The showman, in despair, fled with his charge to the Continent.

Whither he roamed at first I do not know; but he came finally to Brussels. His reception was discouraging. Brussels was firm; the exhibition was banned; it was brutal, indecent and immoral, and could not be permitted within the confines of Belgium. Merrick was thus no longer of value. He was no longer a source of profitable entertainment. He was a burden. He must be got rid of. The elimination of Merrick was a simple matter. He could offer no resistance. He was as docile as a sick sheep. The impresario, having robbed Merrick of his paltry savings, gave him a ticket to London, saw him into the train and no doubt in parting condemned him to perdition. His destination was Liverpool Street.

The journey may be imagined. Merrick was in his alarming outdoor garb. He would be harried by an eager mob as he hobbled along the quay. They would run ahead to get a look at him. They would lift the hem of his cloak to peep at his body. He would try to hide in the train or in some dark corner of the boat, but never could he be free from that ring of curious eyes or from those whispers of fright and aversion. He had but a few shillings in his pocket and nothing either to eat or drink on the way. A panic-dazed dog with a label on his collar would have received some sympathy and possibly some kindness. Merrick received none.

What was he to do when he reached London? He had not a friend in the world. He knew no more of London than he knew of Pekin. How could he find a lodging, or what lodging-house keeper would dream of taking him in? All he wanted was to hide. What most he dreaded were the open street and the gaze of his fellow-men. If even he crept into a cellar the horrid eyes and the still more dreaded whispers would follow him to its depths. Was there ever such a homecoming!

At Liverpool Street he was rescued from the crowd by the police and taken into the third-class waiting-room. Here he sank on the floor in the darkest corner. The police were at a loss what to do with him. They had dealt with strange and mouldy tramps, but never with such an object as this. He could not explain himself. His speech was so maimed that he might as well have spoken in Arabic. He had, however, something with him which he produced with a ray of hope. It was my card. The card simplified matters. It made it evident that this curious creature had an acquaintance and that the individual must be sent for.

A messenger was dispatched to the London Hospital which is comparatively near at hand. Fortunately I was in the building and returned at once with the messenger to the station. In the waiting-room I had some difficulty in making a way through the crowd, but there, on the floor in the corner, was Merrick. He looked a mere heap.

It seemed as if he had been thrown there like a bundle. He was so huddled up and so helpless looking that he might have had both his arms and his legs broken. He seemed pleased to see me, but he was nearly done. The journey and want of food had reduced him to the last stage of exhaustion. The police kindly helped him into a cab, and I drove him at once to the hospital. He appeared to be content, for he fell asleep almost as soon as he was seated and slept to the journey's end. He never said a word, but seemed to be satisfied that all was well.

In the attics of the hospital was an isolation ward with a single bed. It was used for emergency purposes — for a case of delirium tremens, for a man who had become suddenly insane or for a patient with an undetermined fever. Here *The Elephant Man* was deposited on a bed, was made comfortable and was supplied with food. I had been guilty of an irregularity in admitting such a case, for the hospital was neither a refuge nor a home for incurables. Chronic cases were not accepted, but only those requiring active treatment, and Merrick was not in need of such treatment. I applied to the sympathetic chairman of the committee, Mr. Carr Gomm, who not only was good enough to approve my action but who agreed with me that Merrick must not again be turned out into the world.

Mr. Carr-Gomm wrote a letter to the Times detailing the circumstances of the refugee and asking for money for his support. So generous is the English public that in a few days — I think in a week — enough money was forthcoming to maintain Merrick for life. without any charge upon the hospital funds.

There chanced to be two empty rooms at the back of the hospital which were little used. They were on the ground floor, were out of the way, and opened upon a large courtyard called Bedstead Square, because here the iron beds were marshalled for cleaning and painting. The front room was converted into a bed-sitting room and the smaller chamber into a bathroom.

The condition of Merrick's skin rendered a bath at least once a day a necessity, and I might here mention that with the use of the bath the unpleasant odour to which I have referred ceased to be noticeable. Merrick took up his abode in the hospital in December, 1886. Merrick had now something he had never dreamed of, never supposed to be possible — a home of his own for life.

I at once began to make myself acquainted with him and to endeavour to understand his mentality. It was a study of much interest. I very soon learnt his speech so that I could talk freely with him. This afforded him great satisfaction, for, curiously enough, he had a passion for conversation, yet all his life had had no one to talk to. I — having then much leisure — saw him almost every day, and made a point of spending some two hours with him every Sunday morning when he would chatter almost without ceasing. It was unreasonable to expect one nurse to attend to him continuously, but there was no lack of temporary volunteers. As they did not all acquire his speech it came about that I had occasionally to act as an interpreter.

I found Merrick, as I have said, remarkably intelligent. He had learnt to read and had become a most voracious reader. I think he had been taught when he was in hospital with his diseased hip. His range of books was limited. The Bible and Prayer Book he knew intimately, but he had subsisted for the most part upon newspapers, or rather upon such fragments of old journals as he had chanced to pick up. He had read a few stories and some elementary lesson books, but the delight of his life was a romance, especially a love romance. These tales were very real to him, as real as any narrative in the Bible, so that he would tell them to me as incidents in the lives of people who had lived.

In his outlook upon the world he was a child, yet a child with some of the tempestuous feelings of a man. He was an elemental being, so primitive that he might have spent the twenty-three years of his life immured in a cave.

Of his early days I could learn but little. He was very loath to talk about the past. It was a nightmare, the shudder of which was still upon him. He was born, he believed, in or about Of his father he knew absolutely nothing. Of his mother he had some memory. It was very faint and had, I think, been elaborated in his mind into something definite. Mothers figured in the tales he had read, and he wanted his mother to be one of those comfortable lullaby-singing persons who are so loveable. In his subconscious mind there was apparently a germ of recollection in which someone figured who had been kind to him. He clung to this conception and made it more real by invention, for since the day when he could toddle no one had been kind to him. As an infant he must have been repellent, although his deformities did not become gross until he had attained his full stature.

It was a favourite belief of his that his mother was beautiful. The fiction was, I am aware, one of his own making, but it was a great joy to him. His mother, lovely as she may have been, basely deserted him when he was very small, so small that his earliest clear memories were of the work house to which he had been taken. Worthless and inhuman as this mother was, he spoke of her with pride and even with reverence. Once, when referring to his own appearance, he said: "It is very strange, for, you see, mother was so beautiful."

The rest of Merrick's life up to the time that I met him at Liverpool Street Station was one dull record of degradation and squalor. He was dragged from town to town and from fair to fair as if he were a strange beast in a cage. A dozen times a day he would have to expose his nakedness and his piteous deformities before a gaping crowd who greeted him with such mutterings as "Oh! what a horror! What a beast! " He had had no childhood. He had had no boyhood. He had never experienced pleasure. He knew nothing of the joy of living nor of the fun of things. His sole idea of happiness was to creep into the dark and hide.

Shut up alone in a booth, awaiting the next exhibition, how mocking must have sounded the laughter and merriment of the boys and girls outside who were enjoying the "fun of the fair " !

He had no past to look back upon and no future to look forward to. At the age of twenty he was a creature without hope. There was nothing in front of him but a vista of caravans creeping along a road, of rows of glaring show tents and of circles of staring eyes with, at the end, the spectacle of a broken man in a poor law infirmary.

Those who are interested in the evolution of character might speculate as to the effect of this brutish life upon a sensitive and intelligent man. It would be reasonable to surmise that he would become a spiteful and malignant misanthrope, swollen with venom and filled with hatred of his fellow-men, or, on the other hand, that he would degenerate into a despairing melancholic on the verge of idiocy.

Merrick, however, was no such being. He had passed through the fire and had come out unscathed. His troubles had ennobled him. He showed himself to be a gentle, affectionate and loveable creature, as amiable as a happy woman, free from any trace of cynicism or resentment, without a grievance and without an unkind word for anyone. I have never heard him complain. I have never heard him deplore his ruined life or resent the treatment he had received at the hands of callous keepers. His journey through life had been indeed along a via dolorosa, the road had been uphill all the way, and now, when the night was at its blackest and the way most steep, he had suddenly found himself, as it were, in a friendly inn, bright with light and warm with welcome. His gratitude to those about him was pathetic in its sincerity and eloquent in the childlike simplicity with which it was expressed.

As I learnt more of this primitive creature I found that there were two anxieties which were prominent in his mind and which he revealed to me with diffidence. He was in the occupation of the rooms assigned to him and had been assured that he would be cared for to the end of his days. This, however, he found hard to realise, for he often asked me timidly to what place he would next be moved. To understand his attitude it is necessary to remember that he had been moving on and moving on all his life. He knew no other state of existence. To him it was normal. He had passed from the workhouse to the hospital, from the hospital back to the workhouse, then from this town to that town or from one showman's caravan to another. He had never known a home nor any semblance of one. He had no possessions. His sole belongings, besides his clothes and some books, were the monstrous cap and the cloak. He was a wanderer, a pariah and an outcast. That his quarters at the hospital were his for life he could not understand. He could not rid his mind of the anxiety which had pursued him for so many years — where am I to be taken next?

Another trouble was his dread of his fellowmen, his fear of people's eyes, the dread of being always stared at, the lash of the cruel mutterings of the crowd. In his home in Bedstead Square he was secluded; but now and then a thoughtless porter or a ward maid would open his door to let curious friends have a peep at the Elephant Man. It therefore seemed to him as if the gaze of the world followed him still.

Influenced by these two obsessions he became, during his first few weeks at the hospital, curiously uneasy. At last, with much hesitation, he said to me one day: "When I am next moved can I go to a blind asylum or to a lighthouse?" He had read about blind asylums in the newspapers and was. attracted by the thought of being among people who could not see. The lighthouse had another charm. It meant seclusion from the curious. There at least no one could open a door and peep in at him. There he would forget that he had once been *The Elephant Man*. There he would escape the vampire showman. He had never seen a lighthouse, but he had come upon a picture of the Eddystone, and it appeared to him that this lonely column of stone in the waste of the sea was such a home as he had longed for.

I had no great difficulty in ridding Merrick's mind of these ideas. I wanted him to get accustomed to his fellow-men, to become a human being himself and to be admitted to the communion of his kind. He appeared day by day less frightened, less haunted looking, less anxious to hide, less alarmed when he saw his door being opened. He got to know most of the people about the place, to be accustomed to their comings and goings, and to realise that they took no more than a friendly notice of him. He could only go out after dark, and on fine nights ventured to take a walk in Bedstead Square clad in his black cloak and his cap. His greatest adventure was on one moonless evening when he walked alone as far as the hospital garden and back again.

To secure Merrick's recovery and to bring him, as it were, to life once more, it was necessary that he should make the acquaintance of men and women who would treat him as a normal and intelligent young man and not as a monster of deformity. Women I felt to be more important than men in bringing about his transformation. Women were the more frightened of him, the more disgusted at his appearance and the more apt to give way to irrepressible expressions of aversion when they came into his presence. Moreover, Merrick had an admiration of women of such a kind that it attained almost to adoration. This was not the outcome of his personal experience. They were not real women but the products of his imagination. Among them was the beautiful mother surrounded, at a respectful distance, by heroines from the many romances he had read.

His first entry to the hospital was attended by a regrettable incident. He had been placed on the bed in the little attic, and a nurse had been instructed to bring him some food. Unfortunately she had not been fully informed of Merrick's unusual appearance. As she entered the room she saw on the bed, propped up by white pillows, a monstrous figure as hideous as an Indian idol. She at once dropped the tray she was carrying and fled, with a shriek, through the door. Merrick was too weak to notice much, but the experience, I am afraid, was not new to him.

He was looked after by volunteer nurses whose ministrations were somewhat formal and constrained. Merrick, no doubt, was conscious that their service was purely official, that they were merely doing what they were told to do and that they were acting rather as automata than as women. They did not help him to feel that he was of their kind. On the contrary they, without knowing it, made him aware that the gulf of separation was immeasurable.

Feeling this, I asked a friend of mine, a young and pretty widow, if she thought she could enter Merrick's room with a smile, wish him good morning and shake him by the hand. She said she could and she did. The effect upon poor Merrick was not quite what I had expected. As he let go her hand he bent his head on his knees and sobbed until I thought he would never cease. The interview was over. He told me afterwards that this was the first woman who had ever smiled at him, and the first woman, in the whole of his life, who had shaken hands with him. From this day the transformation of Merrick commenced and he began to change, little by little, from a hunted thing into a man. It was a wonderful change to witness and one that never ceased to fascinate me.

Merrick's case attracted much attention in the papers, with the result that he had a constant succession of visitors. Everybody wanted to see him. He must have been visited by almost every lady of note in the social world. They were all good enough to welcome him with a smile and to shake hands with him. The Merrick whom I had found shivering behind a rag of a curtain in an empty shop was now conversant with duchesses and countesses and other ladies of high degree. They brought him presents, made his room bright with ornaments and pictures, and, what pleased him more than all, supplied him with books. He soon had a large library and most of his day was spent in reading. He was not the least spoiled; not the least puffed up; he never asked for anything; never presumed upon the kindness meted out to him, and was always humbly and profoundly grateful.

Above all he lost his shyness. He liked to see his door pushed open and people to look in. He became acquainted with most of the frequenters of Bedstead Square, would chat with them at his window and show them some of his choicest presents. He improved in his speech although to the end his utterances were not easy for strangers to understand. He was beginning, moreover, to be less conscious of his unsightliness, a little disposed to think it was, after all, not so very extreme. Possibly this was aided by the circumstance that I would not allow a mirror of any kind in his room.

The height of his social development was reached on an eventful day when Queen Alexandra — then Princess of Wales — came to the hospital to pay him a special visit. With that kindness which has marked every act of her life, the Queen entered Merrick's room smiling and shook him warmly by the hand. Merrick was transported with delight. This was beyond even his most extravagant dream. The Queen has made many people happy, but I think no gracious act of hers has ever caused such happiness as she brought into Merrick's room when she sat by his chair and talked to him as to a person she was glad to see.

Merrick, I may say, was now one of the most contented creatures I have chanced to meet. More than once he said to me: 'I am happy every hour of the day." This was good to think upon when I recalled the half-dead heap of miserable humanity I had seen in the corner of the waiting-room at Liverpool St. Most men of Merrick's age would have expressed their joy and sense of contentment by singing or whistling when they were alone. Unfortunately poor Merrick's mouth was so deformed that he could neither whistle nor sing. He was satisfied to express himself by beating time upon the pillow to some tune that was ringing in his head. I have many times found him so occupied when I have entered his room unexpectedly.

One thing that always struck me as sad about Merrick was the fact that he could not smile. Whatever his delight might be, his face remained expressionless. He could weep but he could not smile.

The Queen paid Merrick many visits and sent him every year a Christmas card with a message in her own handwriting. On one occasion she sent him a signed photograph of herself. Merrick, quite overcome, regarded it as a sacred object and would hardly allow me to touch it. Pie cried over it, and after it was framed had it put up in his room as a kind of icon. I told him that he must write to Her Royal Highness to thank her for her goodness. This he was pleased to do, as he was very fond of writing letters, never before in his life having had anyone to write to. I allowed the letter to be dispatched unedited. It began "My dear Princess" and ended "Yours very sincerely." Unorthodox as it was it was expressed in terms any courtier would have envied.

Other ladies followed the Queen's gracious example and sent their photographs to this delighted creature who had been all his life despised and rejected of men. His mantelpiece and table became so covered with photographs of handsome ladies, with dainty knickknacks and pretty trifles that they may almost have befitted the apartment of an Adonis-like actor or of a famous tenor.

Through all these bewildering incidents and through the glamour of this great change Merrick still remained in many ways a mere child. He had all the invention of an imaginative boy or girl, the same love of "make-believe," the same instinct of "dressing up" and of personating heroic and impressive characters. This attitude of mind was illustrated by the following incident. Benevolent visitors had given me, from time to time, sums of money to be expended for the comfort of the ci-devant *Elephant Man*. When one Christmas was approaching I asked Merrick what he would like me to purchase as a Christmas present. He rather startled me by saying shyly that he would like a dressing-bag with silver fittings. He had seen a picture of such an article in an advertisement which he had furtively preserved.

The association of a silver-fitted dressing-bag with the poor wretch wrapped up in a dirty blanket in an empty shop was hard to comprehend. I fathomed the mystery in time, for Merrick made little secret of the fancies that haunted his boyish brain. Just as a small girl with a tinsel coronet and a window curtain for a train will realise the conception of a countess on her way to court, so Merrick loved to imagine himself a dandy and a young man about town. Mentally, no doubt, he had frequently "dressed up" for the part. He could "make-believe" with great effect, but he wanted something to render his fancied character more realistic. Hence the jaunty bag which was to assume the function of the toy coronet and the window curtain that could transform a mite with a pigtail into a countess.

As a theatrical "property" the dressing-bag was ingenious, since there was little else to give substance to the transformation. Merrick could not wear the silk hat of the dandy nor, indeed, any kind of hat. He could not adapt his body to the trimly cut coat. His deformity was such that he could wear neither collar nor tie, while in association with his bulbous feet the young blood's patent leather shoe was unthinkable.

What was there left to make up the character? A lady had given him a ring to wear on his undeformed hand, and a noble lord had presented him with a very stylish walking-stick. But these things, helpful as they were, were hardly sufficing. The dressing-bag, however, was distinctive, was explanatory and entirely characteristic. So the bag was obtained and Merrick *The Elephant Man* became, in the seclusion of his chamber, the Piccadilly exquisite, the young spark, the gallant, the "nut."

When I purchased the article, I realised that as 'Merrick could never travel he could hardly want a dressing-bag. He could not use the silver-backed brushes and the comb because he had no hair to brush. The ivory-handled razors were useless because he could not shave. The deformity of his mouth rendered an ordinary toothbrush of no avail, and as his monstrous lips could not hold a cigarette the cigarette-case was a mockery. The silver shoe-horn would be of no service in the putting on of his ungainly slippers, while the hat-brush was quite unsuited to the peaked cap with its visor.

Still the bag was an emblem of the real swell and of the knockabout Don Juan of whom he had read. So every day Merrick laid out upon his table, with proud precision, the silver brushes, the razors, the shoe-horn and the silver cigarette-case which I had taken care to fill with cigarettes. The contemplation of these gave him great pleasure, and such is the power of self-deception that they convinced him he was the "real thing."

I think there was just one shadow in Merrick's life. As I have already said, he had a lively imagination; he was romantic; he cherished an emotional regard for women and his favourite pursuit was the reading of love stories. He fell in love — in a humble and devotional way — with, I think, every attractive lady he saw. He, no doubt, pictured himself the hero of many a passionate incident. His bodily deformity had left unmarred the instincts and feelings of his years. He was amorous. He would like to have been a lover, to have walked with the beloved object in the languorous shades of some beautiful garden and to have poured into her ear all the glowing utterances that he had rehearsed in his heart. And yet — the pity of it — imagine the feelings of such a youth when he saw nothing but a look of horror creep over the face of every girl whose eyes met his. I fancy when he talked of life among the blind there was a half-formed idea in his mind that he might be able to win the affection of a woman if only she were without eyes to see.

As Merrick developed he began to display certain modest ambitions in the direction of improving his mind and enlarging his knowledge of the world. He was as curious as a child and as eager to learn. There were so many things he wanted to know and to see. In the first place he was anxious to view the interior of what he called "a real house," such a house as figured in many of the tales he knew, a house with a hall, a drawing-room where guests were received and a dining-room with plate on the sideboard and with easy chairs into which the hero could "fling himself." The workhouse, the common lodging-house and a variety of mean garrets were all the residences he knew.

To satisfy this wish I drove him up to my small house in Wimpole Street. He was absurdly interested, and examined everything in detail and with untiring curiosity. I could not show him the pampered menials and the powdered footmen of whom he had read, nor could I produce the white marble staircase of the mansion of romance nor the gilded mirrors and the brocaded divans which belong to that style of residence. I explained that the house was a modest dwelling of the Jane Austen type, and as he had read "Emma" he was content.

A more burning ambition of his was to go to the theatre. It was a project very difficult to satisfy. A popular pantomime was then in progress at Drury Lane Theatre, but the problem was how so conspicuous a being as the Elephant Man could be got there, and how he was to see the performance without attracting the notice of the audience and causing a panic or, at least, an unpleasant diversion.

The whole matter was most ingeniously carried through by that kindest of women and most able of actresses — Mrs. Kendal. She made the necessary arrangements with the lessee of the theatre. A box was obtained. Merrick was brought up in a carriage with drawn blinds and was allowed to make use of the royal entrance so as to reach the box by a private stair. I had begged three of the hospital sisters to don evening dress and to sit in the front row in order to "dress " the box, on the one hand, and to form a screen for Merrick on the other. Merrick and I occupied the back of the box which was kept in shadow. All went well, and no one saw a figure, more monstrous than any on the stage, mount the staircase or cross the corridor.

One has often witnessed the unconstrained delight of a child at its first pantomime, but Merrick's rapture was much more intense as well as much more solemn. Here was a being with the brain of a man, the fancies of a youth and the imagination of a child. His attitude was not so much that of delight as of wonder and amazement. He was awed. He was enthralled. The spectacle left him speechless, so that if he were spoken to he took no heed. He often seemed to be panting for breath. I could not help comparing him with a man of his own age in the stalls. This satiated individual was bored to distraction, would look wearily at the stage from time to time and then yawn as if he had not slept for nights ; while at the same time Merrick was thrilled by a vision that was almost beyond his comprehension.

Merrick talked of this pantomime for weeks and weeks. To him, as to a child with the faculty of make-believe, everything was real; the palace was the home of kings, the princess was of royal blood, the fairies were as undoubted as the children in the street, while the dishes at the banquet were of unquestionable gold. He did not like to discuss it as a play but rather as a vision of some actual world. When this mood possessed him he would say: "I wonder what the prince did after we left," or "Do you think that poor man is still in the dungeon?" and so on and so on.

The splendour and display impressed him, but, I think, the ladies of the ballet took a still greater hold upon his fancy. He did not like the ogres and the giants, while the funny men impressed him as irreverent. Having no experience as a boy of romping and ragging, of practical jokes or of "larks," he had little sympathy with the doings of the clown, but, I think (moved by some mischievous instinct in his subconscious mind), he was pleased when the policeman was smacked in the face, knocked down and generally rendered undignified.

Later on another longing stirred the depths of Merrick's mind. It was a desire to see the country, a desire to live in some green secluded spot and there learn something about flowers and the ways of animals and birds. The country as viewed from a wagon on a dusty high road was all the country he knew. He had never wandered among the fields nor followed the windings of a wood. He had never climbed to the brow of a breezy down. He had never gathered flowers in a meadow. Since so much of his reading dealt with country life he was possessed by the wish to see the wonders of that life himself.

This involved a difficulty greater than that presented by a visit to the theatre. The project was, however, made possible on this occasion also by the kindness and generosity of a lady — Lady Knightley — who offered Merrick a holiday home in a cottage on her estate. Merrick was conveyed to the railway station in the usual way, but as he could hardly venture to appear on the platform the railway authorities were good enough to run a second-class carriage into a distant siding. To this point Merrick was driven and was placed in the carriage unobserved. The carriage, with the curtains drawn, was then attached to the main line train.

He duly arrived at the cottage, but the house wife (like the nurse at the hospital) had not been made clearly aware of the unfortunate man's appearance. Thus it happened that when Merrick presented himself, his hostess, throwing her apron over her head, fled, gasping, to the fields. She affirmed that such a guest was beyond her powers of endurance.

Merrick was then conveyed to a gamekeeper's cottage which was hidden from view and was close to the margin of a wood. The man and his wife were able to tolerate his presence. They treated him with the greatest kindness, and with them he spent the one supreme holiday of his life. He could roam where he pleased. He met no one on his wanderings, for the wood was preserved and denied to all but the gamekeeper and the forester.

There is no doubt that Merrick passed in this retreat the happiest time he had as yet experienced. He was alone in a land of wonders. The breath of the country passed over him like a healing wind. Into the silence of the wood the fearsome voice of the showman could never penetrate. No cruel eyes could peep at him through the friendly undergrowth. It seemed as if in this place of peace all stain had been wiped away from his sullied past. The Merrick who had once crouched terrified in the filthy shadows of a Mile End shop was now sitting in the sun, in a clearing among the trees, arranging a bunch of violets he had gathered.

His letters to me were the letters of a delighted and enthusiastic child. He gave an account of his trivial adventures, of the amazing things he had seen, and of the beautiful sounds he had heard. He had met with strange birds, had startled a hare from her form, had made friends with a fierce dog, and had watched the trout darting in a stream. He sent me some of the wild flowers he had picked. They were of the commonest and most familiar kind, but they were evidently regarded by him as rare and precious specimens. He came back to London, to his quarters in Bedstead Square, much improved in health, pleased to be "home" again and to be once more among his books, his treasures and his many friends.

Some six months after Merrick's return from the country he was found dead in bed. This was in April, 1890. He was lying on his back as if asleep, and had evidently died suddenly and without a struggle, since not even the coverlet of the bed was disturbed. The method of his death was peculiar. So large and so heavy was his head that he could not sleep lying down. When he assumed the recumbent position the massive skull was inclined to drop backwards, with the result that he experienced no little distress. The attitude he was compelled to assume when he slept was very strange. He sat up in bed with his back supported by pillows, his knees were drawn up, and his arms clasped round his legs, while his head rested on the points of his bent knees.

He often said to me that he wished he could lie down to sleep "like other people." I think on this last night he must, with some determination, have made the experiment. The pillow was soft, and the head, when placed on it, must have fallen backwards and caused a dislocation of the neck. Thus it came about that his death was due to the desire that had dominated his life — the pathetic but hopeless desire to be "like other people."

As a specimen of humanity, Merrick was ignoble and repulsive; but the spirit of Merrick, if it could be seen in the form of the living, would assume the figure of an upstanding and heroic man, smooth browed and clean of limb, and with eyes that flashed undaunted courage. His tortured journey had come to an end.

All the way he, like another, had borne on his back a burden almost too grievous to bear. He had been plunged into the Slough of Despond, but with manly steps had gained the farther shore. He had been made "a spectacle to all men" in the heartless streets of Vanity Fair. He had been ill-treated and reviled and bespattered with the mud of Disdain. He had escaped the clutches of the

Giant Despair, and at last had reached the "Place of Deliverance," where "his burden loosed from off his shoulders and fell from off his back, so that he saw it no more."

APPENDIX F

THE PENNY SHOWMAN
By Tom Norman

Extracts from the series of weekly articles written by Tom Norman, *The Silver King,* for the showman's weekly journal, The World's Fair. Pages 102 to 109

It was the latter part of November 1884 on a Thursday, I believe. Professor Durland was with me, showing the *Man-Fish* and *Transparent Lady*. The Professor was due to leave on the Sunday to open at the East India Dock Road premises, replacing the *Danlo Sisters* (contortion and acrobatics) due to appear elsewhere. Now I had *Osmondo* and *Solonika* (Second sight) ready to open in the Whitechapel shop if required. I had been in correspondence with Mr. George Hitchcock (*Little George*) and had agreed to take over the management of *The Elephant Man*, Joseph Meyrick. That is how I read the name shown to me on what I believe was the release form issued by the Leicester Infirmary - later in newspaper articles the name was spelt Merrick - but no matter.

I had expected *Little George* and Merrick to arrive the previous day and was glad I had a novelty to show next week in case of a slip-up. It was later afternoon when they arrived. The show was open and the professor was well able to carry on without me. Joseph was a short man and well muffled up in long black coat, black felt hat, with a woolen muffler up to his eyes. *Little George* introduced Merrick as Joe who removed the hat, coat, etc and I saw him for the first time. I had seen many curious people before, some really repulsive, so I had taught myself to control my features - but I hadn't expected this. I remember thinking, 'Oh God! I can't use you'. But on looking into this unfortunate man's eyes I could see so much suffering and pleading that a great feeling of pity and sympathy overcame any other emotions I may have had. I shook his hand and tried to put him at ease, and said, 'Well, Mr. Merrick, I'll call you Joseph if I may,' trying to impart that little dignity that the full name of Joseph has over 'Joe'. But I must confess had I met Joseph in the workhouse I would never have been a party to his release.

I hope I am not doing you an injustice, George, but it occurred to me that the others and yourself had accepted responsibility for Joseph - put him on show at a couple or so towns in the Midlands, probably with no great success - sought to pass your problem onto me. However, I had signed the agreement and was now involved and decided to make the best of the situation. When *Little George* and Joseph parted that day I could see there was a spirit of friendship between them. This certainly disposed of the lie contained in the letter in the Times by the chairman of the London Hospital stating that *The Elephant Man* 'was dragged about from town to town, and from fair to fair, and lived a life that was little better than dismal slavery - he was not treated with actual unkindness, but lived a life of almost solitary confinement....' How anyone can reconcile these two contradictory statements is a mystery to me. as for the dragging from fair to fair - to the best of my knowledge Joseph never saw the inside of a caravan, and I never met any showman who would say different. I cannot, of course, vouch for anything that happened after they took Joseph away.

However, back to the show. I at once tried to make Joseph feel at ease, and already the look of apprehension was gone from his eyes. On occasions I have had to 'rough it', but only through necessity. I do like a bit of comfort and, above all, cleanliness - which was a must in any of my father's butchers shops - my assistant sweeping out every morning. I had installed a large size gas ring, surrounded by bricks to conserve the heat. This was a good source of warmth and boiling the kettle, etc. I had two small iron beds, one for myself and the other for any of my novelties who cared to use it. I sent my assistant (little Jimmy, a bright lad about 12 years of age) with 7/6 [seven shillings and sixpence] round to Blundells for a new mattress and a couple of blankets. These I put on Joseph's bed - this little action was much appreciated by him - more so when I fitted up the curtain around his bed so he had a bit of privacy.

Professor Durland left the show on Sunday night and Joseph and I opened up around mid-day Monday, I had been left some rather crude posters depicting some monster half-man half-elephant rampaging through the jungle. I'm afraid poor Joseph was not capable of much more than a somewhat erratic walk - I must admit I would often indulge in the 'showman's license' when trying to get the people in, whatever show I had. But to make extravagant claims on the outside of the show which you were unable to some extent to justify inside, would only alienate the audience and give them the feeling of being 'HAD'. Therefore, pointing to the illustrations, I would explain they were shown only to arouse interest. *'The Elephant Man* is not here to frighten you but to enlighten you, but I would like to stress that ladies in a Delicate State of Health are advised not to attend'.

It had been stated in various writings that Joseph was exhibited and treated like a wild animal. I believe that most of the show's visitors, after the shock of seeing Joseph, must have felt some sympathy and pity for him, and had I attempted to be harsh with him in front of the audience, I would very soon have had the show wrecked, and me with it.

From the earliest days as a novelty showman I always addressed my audience with the same opening sentence, which gave me a little 'leeway' and was my excuse against any awkward questions from the more inquisitive members that may be present:

Ladies and gentleman, IN THE ABSENCE OF THE LECTURER with your indulgence I would like to introduce Mr. Joseph

Merrick, the Elephant Man. Before doing so I ask you please to prepare yourselves - Brace yourselves up to witness one who is probably the most remarkable human being ever to draw the breath of life.

Upon opening the curtains there was always the gasp of horror and shock, and sometimes the hurried exit of one or more of the audience. I would continue with the tale thus:

Ladies and gentleman, I ask you please not to despise or condemn this man on account of his unusual appearance. Remember we do not make ourselves, and were you to cut or prick Joseph he would bleed, and that bleed or blood would be red, the same as yours or mine.

I went on to explain how the unfortunate man's mother had been frightened by an elephant when in a Delicate State of Health, and gave birth to Joseph some time after, and how Joseph, an intelligent man, having become somewhat of a burden to his family, had been put into the Leicester Workhouse. But Joseph, not content to live off charity, seized the opportunity of joining the showmen who secured his release, and was now able to pay his way and be independent of charity.

As a showman it was my job to, 'Tell the Tale' outside and get the customers inside, and send them out satisfied with what they had seen. Every businessman knows, whether it be Harrods or the little corner shop, a satisfied customer may tell his friends, but a dissatisfied customer tells everybody. Besides several posters, I had been left about 1000 pamphlets to be sold at 1/2d each at the end of the show. These gave a short outline concerning the life of *The Elephant Man*, all the proceeds to go to Joseph Merrick. The selling of these gave me an extra reason to please the audience. The pamphlets sold very well. I had got the audience on our side. Although they could not have admired his appearance, none could doubt his spirit. The takings at the door were quite good, and we were both satisfied in that respect. We had a bit of 'rough and ready' comfort, and I know Joseph was quite content and said, 'I don't ever want to go back to that place' (the workhouse).

It was in the early hours of one morning, about a week after Joseph's arrival, that I got out of bed for some reason I now forget. The curtain around Joseph's bed was partly open and I saw he was sitting up in bed with his chin resting on his knees. I asked if he felt ill, he said he was alright and always slept in that position. To lie down flat would be very risky, as he put it: 'I might wake up with a broken neck'. I thought some support for his head should be possible, such as the yoke the girls wore on the farms for carrying the milk pails. I decided I would do something about it.

One morning just as we were opening the shop a young man approached me and introduced himself as Dr Tuckett. His manner was most respectful and pleasant. He seemed genuinely interesting in meeting *The Elephant Man* and, in an apologetic way, asked if it would be possible for him to meet Joseph before the show opened for business. I liked this young man's appearance and straight away introduced him to Joseph. The three of us had quite an interesting conversation for several minutes, during which time we discovered that we all had something in common - we were all around 24 years of age. Upon leaving, Dr. Tuckett asked me if I could kindly extend the privilege he had himself received to a colleague from the hospital -- Mr. Treves, who would attend before the shop was open, so as not to obstruct the business. Had I only known at the time the trouble, antagonism and abuse that man caused me, my answer would definitely have been quite different, and I would not have agreed to Mr. Treves at that time or any other.

May I at this point revert to my 'manager' (*Little Jimmy*). The first thing I impressed upon his mind when he joined my staff was that if anybody - ANYBODY - asked him any questions about myself, Joseph or the show he must always answer, 'I don't know'. I also devised a secret whistle which he was to give if he saw a policeman approaching when I was causing obstructions outside the show, or he wished to attract my attention for any reason, with a call-sign that would pass un-noticed by persons 'not in the know'. This intrigued Jimmy greatly. The signal composed of whistling the lower note on the music scale immediately following this with the top note, much the same as a donkey's 'HEE-HAW' in reverse. This whistle the family in after years always used, and was useful in many ways and on numerous occasions.

I Meet Dr. Treves

It was on a morning shortly after Dr. Tuckett's visit. I was in the coffee house buying the breakfast for Joseph and myself when, from a short distance away, I heard the Whistle. Although I had put up a thick pair of curtains to the door of the shop for easier passage when we were open, Jimmy had pulled the door to, but not having the key to lock it, had only accompanied our visitor just far enough to point out where I was and hurried back to his post. I believe this was about the last week in November '84, and it's just come to me.

I remember that the coffee house was run by a man by the name of Jack Winders which is, I suppose, not very important. But I like to keep the record straight. Anyway, this rather important-looking man (who certainly looked, and I am sure by his attitude felt, out of place in this somewhat dingy place of refreshment) approached me and said - somewhat offensively I thought - 'Are you Norman the Showman?' 'That is my name, sir, unfortunately.' This word 'unfortunately' I always included whenever addressed by name by someone unknown to me. This I had found was a good way of 'Breaking the Ice' and making contact, as it invariably begat the question 'Why unfortunately?' The answer to this was, of course, 'I sometimes wish I was someone else' or some such nonsense. Anyway it was, I thought, always a neat way to start the conversation going and get to business.

Dr. Treves however ignored my 'gag'. He, probably having very little sense of humour, was anxious to get out. But I was not going to be hurried by him and suggested if he didn't like the atmosphere he could wait outside until my order was ready. This was probably a pair of bloaters or kippers, a large jug of tea, coffee or cocoa and half a dozen 'doorsteps' (thick slices of bread). These we could fry in the pan, toast or smother with dripping, butter or whatever Joseph and I fancied. I was aware that the doctor was annoyed at being kept waiting. I did not like the man, but thinking he could probably do me a bit of good, or perhaps no good, I was as quick as possible to conduct him to the show.

I am not going into details regards Dr. Treves' conversation and examination of Joseph, allowing him at least 15 minutes - explaining to him that we both were ready for our breakfast. After the doctor had left we had our meal, in which Jimmy shared and said, 'He didn't half want to know a lot, Guv'nor - about Mr. Merrick and you, and if you were friendly. But I kept saying, 'I don't know' like you told me. Then the man said, 'You don't know much, do you?' so I told him I did know where Mr. Norman was, but wouldn't tell him for less than sixpence - which I got'. At this point I would like to quote from the written account Dr. Treves gave of his meeting with *The Elephant Man* and the surroundings in which he found him:-

'the shop was empty and grey with dust. Some old tins and a few shriveled potatoes occupied a shelf, and some vague vegetable refuse in the window....'

To deal with this statement first - Jimmy's first job every morning was to sweep out. There was no shelf. There had been a platform top in the window, but before I even opened the shop I had taken this down to make more room for the audience, and I utilised it to make a low stage for Joseph, It must be obvious that it would be dangerous to have left it, when members of the audience would surely clamber on to it to get a better view when the shop was full - with the inevitable collapse of the structure, and the possible result of injuries. Dr. Treves again: -

'the room was cold and dank, for it was the month of November...'

For myself I agree it was November, but that does not signify that indoors had to be cold and dank.

Dr. Treves:- *'The showman pulled back the curtain and revealed a bent figure crouching on a stool, and covered by a brown blanket. In front of it, on a tripod, was a large brick heated by a Bunsen burner....'*

My reply - Dr. Treves states that the shop was cold and dank, and lit by the faint blue light of the gas jet. Yet he was able to note and record that there was a red tablecloth and a brown blanket. He must have possessed very good eyesight and equally good memory. I myself do not remember which colours these were, so it's possible he described them correctly.

Dr. Treves 'heated by a Bunsen Burner' - my reply: It is quite possible that at that time I never knew what a Bunsen Burner was. Anyway, with our rather crude method of heating it wasn't ideal, but it was really cosy. I had roughed it at times, but I liked a bit of comfort and always tried to achieve it. I envy the doctor on one account only - his mastery of prose and his ability to dramatise the situation thus:-

'This hunched up figure was the embodiment of loneliness. It might have been a captive in a cavern, or a wizard watching for unholy manifestations in the ghostly flame....' (the Bunsen Burner).

He seemed a bit undecided. However he does state that the sun was shining outside. Many years ago at school I remember learning the words of some poet or other:-

*'Words are like leaves, and where they most abound
Much fruit of sense is very rarely found.'*

I admit that to apply this quotation to the greatly respected and talented Dr. Treves must appear to his friends akin to blasphemy. I am really at a loss to account for that man's antagonism towards me. In his writings he states:-

'The Showman, speaking as to a dog, called out harshly, 'Stand up'. The thing arose slowly letting the blanket that covered its head and black fall to the ground. There stood the most disgusting specimen of humanity that I have ever seen....'

I'm afraid I am unable to imagine Dr. Treves was a very compassionate or sympathetic person, and he was not slow some time later to take advantage of the publicity, and pose as the Guardian Angel of this 'thing' that he found 'repulsive and disgusting'.

Shortly after the visit by Dr. Treves a far more welcome visitor (Dr. Tuckett) enquired if I would be willing to allow Joseph to attend the hospital, and appear before a group of medical people. Joseph was quite agreeable to this, and thinking a bit of publicity would do me no harm, and their medical attention might do Joseph a bit of good. I am not sure if it was after the second or third of these visits that Joseph said he did not wish to go again.

He had no objection to being on show, presented in a decent manner and getting paid for it, 'But over there I was stripped naked, and felt like an animal at a cattle market'.

It was about a week later when I was asked to allow Joseph to go over to the hospital and I refused. Dr. Treves himself came over immediately and claimed he had several distinguished visitors that he had invited to meet the Elephant Man. The doctor appeared almost desperate, afraid, I imagine of 'losing face' among his colleagues. I kept the doctor waiting whilst I advised Joseph of the situation. I myself would have liked him to go, but by this time I had learned that, despite his disability, he had a will of his own. So when he refused I made no attempt to coerce him. I could see that Dr. Treves could hardly control his rage at being told of Joseph's refusal especially when I said that in future he and his colleagues could only see Joseph as paying customers. The good doctor of course concluded that this was all my doing and that was the start of the campaign of vilification against me. I am convinced that he was instrumental for the authorities ultimately closing the show. Remember I was very young at the time, and without much experience. Later on in life they would have found me a rather harder 'nut to crack'.

Much more I could write about the bond between Joseph and myself. He was a man of very strong character and beliefs - anxious to earn his own living and be independent of charity. To give just one instance of this was disclosed only a day or so before we parted. In my early career as a Showman I always had a cheap print-photo of whichever novelty of 'freak' I had on show. If not a photo I would have printed a small pamphlet giving details etc to sell at the end of each show. A fellow Showman who came and saw the show commented on the fact that I had no 'sellings'. (We had sold all of Joseph's pamphlets - more were on order), and suggested we should work the 'Nobbings'. This meant going around with the hat and collecting for the 'Benefit of the Performer' or whatever novelty was on show. I had never done this before. Joseph was with us when this suggestion was made. He immediately turned to me and said, "We are not beggars are we, Thomas?" This, coming from a man who had always experienced 'hard times' and was anxious to get as much money as he could, struck me as a 'noble gesture' and one that increased my admiration for this poor misshapen man.

A few days later I had to admit defeat. The opposition had won. The partnership was broken up and Joseph was taken away. I often think that I was the only real friend Joseph ever had, and had come to share his ambition which was only to save enough money and find him a home somewhere. I believe he would have achieved that wish had they left him with me. I don't want to dwell on the parting of Joseph and myself. Suffice to say it was not a happy one for Joseph. But for Dr. Treves to put in print that "The Showman, in despair, fled with his charge to the continent" is a lie, or he was wrongly misinformed. It is on record that when *The Elephant Man* was taken from me he had £50 in his possession. It was in fact considerably more. He regularly received his share of the takings. This, in fact, was more than I had, having to pay the rent, gas, food, etc. Anyway, if it was only £50 that was far more than I had at that time, and a great many times since.

After Joseph's departure I thought I had seen the last of him, which indeed I had, but some months later, I heard that Joseph had found 'sanctuary' in the London Hospital. One day, in answer to a note brought to me by a porter at the hospital, known as Jack (Simmons) I believe, I went to the hospital to see Joseph but was refused admission. I did not again make the attempt. I had been persecuted often enough through my association with him, and had no wish to revive the issue. The porter, Jack, a few weeks later left the hospital to return to Ireland.

APPENDIX G

FREDERICK TREVES vs TOM NORMAN: ANOTHER PERSPECTIVE
Gerry LeFurgy, Historian, FoJCM

I gratefully acknowledge the contributions of Audrey Kantrowitz, Mae Siu Wai Stroshane, both of the United States and Jeanette Sitton, of London, England, United Kingdom.

In examining the differences between Sir Frederick Treves' and Tom Norman's recollections of Joseph Merrick, *The Elephant Man*, in their respective memoirs, I have long maintained that when reading them, one must keep in mind this of their disparate points of view on the facts, of Joseph, and what each inferred of the other.

Treves had more to gain by writing his recollections of Joseph the way he did; Tom Norman had more to lose if he hadn't written his recollections as they appeared.

Treves knew that as a professional and 'respectable' man of the English upper-class, posterity would accord his version of Joseph's life more respect and credibility than the alternate 'competitor' for Joseph's story, the 'lowly showman', Tom Norman. There is no doubt that Treves did come to have genuine compassion for Joseph, but his concern when relating his association with *The Elephant Man* appears to come across as the 'saviour' of helpless Joseph. The main criticism of his association of Joseph, he likely suspected, would be that he had used him solely for his own purposes, to make a name for himself in the world of science and medicine. This was indeed part of his original motive and there was nothing wrong in that. This is how human progress of any kind moves forward. He was also genuinely concerned about Joseph as a patient, and later, as a human being.

But the evidence subtly points out a number of things which call into question his recollections. In his memoirs, Treves described bringing Joseph to his home and the latter felt 'let down' at not seeing something grander, (ie. the powdered footmen), having allegedly stated always wanting to see a 'real home'. Treves stressed the naivety of Joseph, stating he had very childlike impressions of other people and the world at large.[1]

Whilst Joseph may have been 'hoping' to see something grander when he visited, the facts strongly indicate Treves exaggerated this deliberately. Joseph would have known better. How? The fact was, *The Elephant Man* had been a 'hawker' as a youth, (door to door salesman). He would have known the difference between the estates he read about in novels and what he was actually realistically going to encounter at Treves' home, (probably a lot like the homes of what he'd knocked on the doors of, as a youth).[2]

So while Joseph likely was 'trusting', and perhaps even gullible, to some degree, he was no loopy dreamer on the day of his domestic visit, or at any other point in time. It appears that Treves embellishes to serve this purpose; to make his account of Joseph the one to be more likely believed than that of his main competitor, Tom Norman.

And in this vein, Treves completely pulls the wool over our eyes when it comes to the evidence; Joseph was anything but naive and childlike when dealing with people.[3]

The Elephant Man had a huge amount of life experience in dealing with people in a vast array of circumstances, from every class, culture, nationality, etc. Joseph Merrick knew full well the difference between fantasy and reality; the fact he survived to the age he did proves it. Consider just a few things from his life.

- How he attended school with other children in Leicester.

- How he presumably helped out in both his parents' haberdashery store and his uncle's barber shop.

- How he had to 'get along' with his step family and then his uncle's family after several intense life changes.

- Working in a cigar factory.

- While working as a street hawker, Joseph would have travelled all over Leicester and dealt with people of all walks of life.

- Twice, he enrolled himself in the workhouse and had to deal with all the people, (and their associated hang-ups/authority figures, etc), while there.

- He went out of his way to contact Sam Torr and carve out a career for himself as a sideshow attraction.[4]

Even before becoming a sideshow attraction, *The Elephant Man's* life points to an individual with a huge amount of experience dealing with people in very vast life situations. It begs the question: How could Joseph have survived, no matter how much benevolence he may have received, if he hadn't possessed a practicable set of social skills, (such as the ability to 'read' and deal with people)?

The sideshow career would have expanded his life experiences and social skills even more. For there, he would had to have dealt with all manner of people in all manner of roles, (i.e., innkeepers, grocers, circus management and payroll, other performers of all nationalities, people of every background and social strata who came to the carnival). Constantly on the move, dealing with new persons every day, there is simply no way Joseph could have lived this life and not had a firm grip on reality, understanding of human nature and people skills. In my opinion, it's just impossible. Bertram Dooley, the Irish boxer who acted as Joseph's bodyguard at the orders of Sam Torr, later remarked of Joseph that he was always very impressed with the high quality of conversation they'd enjoyed together.[5] This strongly suggests that if Joseph had such interactions with Dooley, is it not reasonable to assume that he could and did do so with others? Shy and quiet, Joseph Carey Merrick certainly was, but not infantile and ignorant. And the latest documentary made about his life verifies that *The Elephant Man's* speech, if afflicted to some degree on account of his deformity, was nevertheless more than coherent.[6]

And when Merrick settled at the London Hospital, there as well, he dealt with people from all manner of walks of life, from the tradesmen in Bedstead Square to the Royal Family.[7] Even his insight of wanting to go to a blind asylum to find a female partner demonstrates a man who had a firm grip on the reality of his situation and of people.[8] So in this regard, Frederick Treves distracted completely the plain and obvious facts: There is no way *The Elephant Man* could have lived the life which he verifiably did and have been the unworldly and naive person which the doctor portrayed him as.

On the other hand, when we compare Treves' and Tom Norman's accounts, we should keep in mind that if in doing so, we come to dislike Treves' apparently haughty demeanour, it does not necessarily follow that his account is false or inherently less credible than Norman's. As well, we must not fall prey to the logical fallacy of, 'Myth of the Middle Ground': It is always a logical err to conclude, given two disparate points of view, the truth must be somewhere in the middle, for no other reason than it is the middle position. The truth may very well be somewhere in the middle, but it could also be somewhere totally else. Both parties could be completely wrong or even, one party can be 100% correct. There must be independent evidence to suggest that the middle position is in fact correct.

With regards to Tom Norman's unpublished memoirs,[9] when he compiled them it was likely he was aware that, as a member of the lower classes and holding an occupation which would never be deemed as 'respectable' by the social betters, he would never be allotted the same credibility as Treves'. The *Silver King* was running an unfair race against the good doctor in this regard and he knew it.

An objective examination of his memoirs strongly suggests that he too, wrote with points of exaggeration, not only to 'take a swipe' back at Treves, (though this was also a priority), but to 'angle' his version in the best possible manner. He knew that he could never gain as much from his past with Joseph in the manner which Treves could and did. Regardless of the fact that Joseph had done very well as a result of their partnership, (for example, having made a very considerable sum of money),[10] the best Norman could hope for was to 'minimise' the negative image which he knew would be painted of him as the 'exploitative and unscrupulous manager' by the man of the 'establishment', Dr. Frederick Treves. To this end, he, too, occluded the facts about Joseph's nature.

Let us consider; if Joseph well and truly disliked Treves', personally, and the entire experience of their initial examination and the resulting presentation to the Pathological Society in 1884,[11] (Norman claimed Joseph said he was 'treated like cattle' thereat), then why did Joseph retain Treves' card?[12] What obvious attachment would he have had to Treves that would inspire him to do this?

The facts we know of his life compel us to accept that, for the most part, Joseph was a good judge of people. If his initial experience of Treves had been as unpleasant as Norman depicts, then Joseph's reaction to being told that there were no answers to his condition, (or hope for a cure), would have been to discard Treves' card and put the entire experience behind him, (much as he did with the first doctor to ever officially examine him, Dr. Marriott of the Leicester Union Infirmary, the surgeon who removed the tumour from Joseph's upper lip in 1882).[13] But he didn't; the card was produced at the train station and this saved his life. Norman's account in this regard does not square with the facts.

In sum, both Frederick Treves and Tom Norman wrote their accounts of Joseph Merrick, *The Elephant Man*, with particular concerns motivating them. The former had something to gain by making his charge appear as 'helpless as a newborn babe', and thereby make his intervention appear even more noble than the immense amount it was; the latter to both provide an angry and rightful self-justification and to minimise undeserved criticism. Let us be critical and thoughtful when we discern historical evidence.

Footnotes:

[1] Treves, Frederick, *The Elephant Man and Other Reminiscences*, in Howell, Michael, & Ford, Peter. *The True History of the Elephant Man* (Allison & Busby, 1992), p. 196
[2] Howell, Michael, & Ford, Peter. *The True History of the Elephant Man* (Allison & Busby, 1992), p. 49
[3] Ibid., p.188
[4] Ibid., p. 62
[5] Ibid., p. 80
[6] *Meet the Elephant Man*, Discovery Health TV documentary, first aired March 23, 2011 (Windfall Films, 2011)
[7] Howell, Michael, & Ford, Peter. *The True History of the Elephant Man*. (Allison & Busby, 1992), p. 192
[8] Ibid., p. 196
[9] Ibid., p. 65
[10] Ibid., p. 85
[11] Ibid., p. 77
[12] Treves, Frederick, *The Elephant Man and Other Reminiscences*, in Howell, Michael, & Ford, Peter. *The True History of the Elephant Man*, (Allison & Busby, 1992), p. 186
[13] Howell & Ford, *The True History of the Elephant Man*

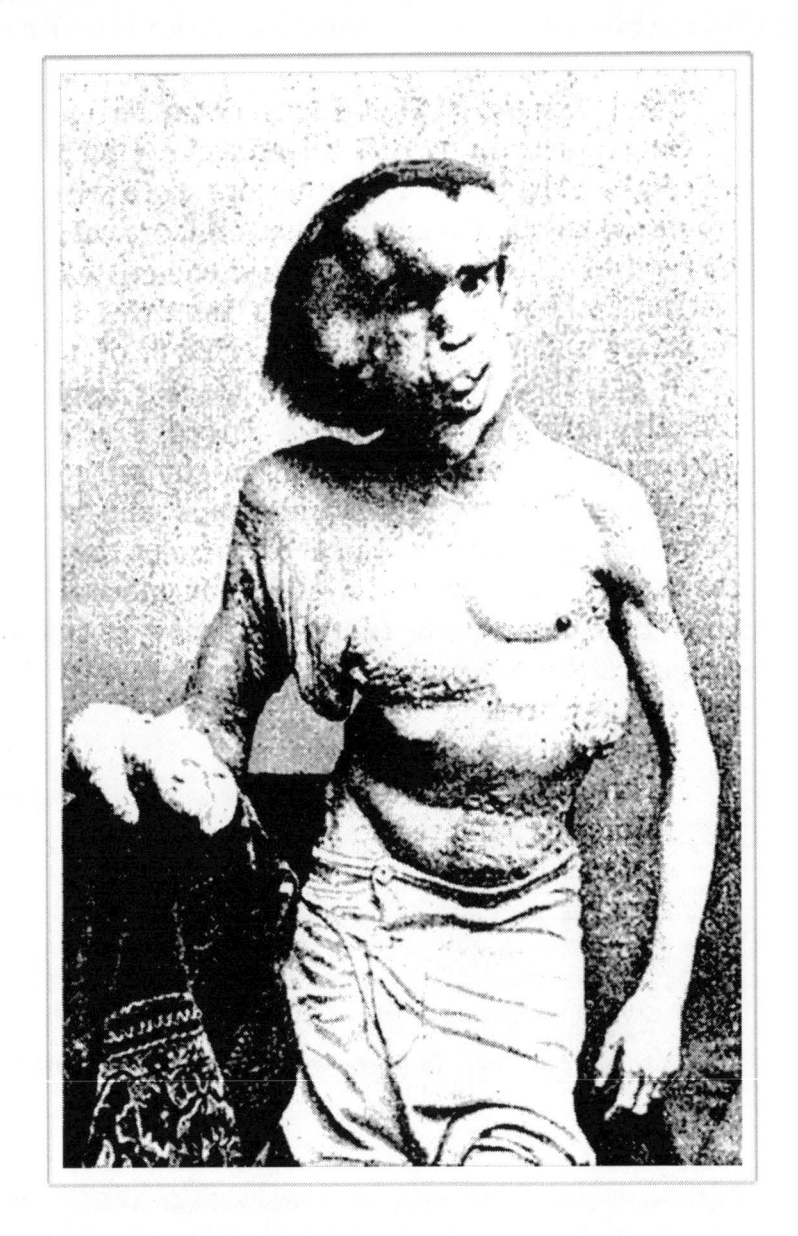

Joseph Merrick in 1889. (Frederick Treves) (Public domain)

APPENDIX H

JOSEPH CAREY MERRICK: PATIENT BY ANOTHER NAME

By Jonathan Evans, Archivist
The Royal London Hospital Archives and Museum

Without doubt Joseph Merrick, the so-called *Elephant Man*, has become the best-known patient of the London (now Royal London) Hospital, past or present. He lived in the hospital for nearly four years, from June 1886 until his death in April 1890, and so qualifies as one of the longest-staying patients in the hospital's history.

Today, most people know Joseph by another name, however, since many encountered his story through watching the film *The Elephant Man*, directed by David Lynch, which appeared in 1980, or perhaps even through seeing the award-winning play of the same name, by Bernard Pomerance, first staged in London two years earlier. In these fictional works the character of the title is called 'John Merrick', a name which derives from a memoir by the London Hospital surgeon Sir Frederick Treves, which appeared in a book entitled *The Elephant Man and Other Reminiscences*, published by Cassell & Co.in 1923.

Treves' story about his rescue of the deformed and destitute Merrick remains an absorbing account. Late in life, Sir Frederick had planned and then abandoned a project to publish an autobiography, featuring his famous patients, who included King Edward VII, who had died in 1910. Treves had performed a successful operation to relieve the King's appendicitis at Buckingham Palace in1902. Instead, Treves decided to write about what he termed his: "queer unknown patients, from the great army of suffering men and women I've been mixed up with". His book of reminiscences includes an essay entitled *The*

Old Receiving Room about the Casualty Department at the London Hospital and elements of that story were woven into the screenplay for David Lynch's film *The Elephant Man*.

In the film the nature of Joseph's deformities (graphically portrayed by the actor John Hurt) are shown with anatomical accuracy; picture research ensures that the film depicts the hospital's wards with historical authenticity and yet the film-makers, in common with the playwrights (several plays have been written) choose to perpetuate the myth that Joseph Merrick was called 'John' in spite of the plentiful historical evidence to the contrary.

The manuscript of Frederick Treves' last book was sold by its British owners in the 1980s and is now in the United States, but before an export licence was granted, photocopies were taken and one of these was deposited with the Royal London Hospital Archives and Museum. The manuscript indicates that Treves wrote at the first instance, with minimal alterations. He originally entered Merrick's first name as 'Joseph', but deleted it and substituted the name 'John'. Writers have conjectured the reasons for this change of name: some have said Treves' memory failed him, the book having been written just a few months before his death and at a time when his health was failing. Moreover, the events described had taken place more than 30 years earlier and Treves mixes up facts contained in some other reminiscences contained in the book. It has also been argued that the form of Joseph's mouth and lips would have made it difficult for him to enunciate clearly and that Treves may have misheard his name. Overgrowth of bone and flesh from Joseph's upper lip had been excised some years earlier at Leicester Infirmary and his remaining teeth were probably extracted at the same time.

Another theory conjectures that Treves, a devout Christian, was eager to avoid any associations between Merrick, who Treves believed to be suffering from a congenital disease, and fatherhood and therefore he changed Joseph's name to John to disassociate him from the paternal associations that the name Joseph has for Christians.

None of these explanations appears totally convincing: Treves had met Joseph on a very regular basis for four years and would have come across a pamphlet entitled *'The life and adventures of Joseph Carey Merrick...half a man and half an elephant'* which was sold at the show where he was exhibited. Whilst Treves' memory might not have been what it was, his writing in his final published work is lucid and many regard it as his best non-medical book. Treves' Christian beliefs had not prevented him from writing Merrick's name correctly during Joseph's lifetime. It seems more likely that Treves named Merrick 'John' by changing Joseph's forename, Treves was affording his former patient at least a modicum of anonymity and making his breach of doctor / patient confidentiality less marked. Additionally, 'John' suited the character of the man he was portraying in his story: someone who was previously traumatised and unable to express himself, but who was able to do so with the help of Treves and his hospital colleagues.

This theme is poignantly made in the film, which also crucially alters the facts and the sequence of events so that Merrick is inaccurately portrayed as being abducted from the Hospital and taken to the Continent after being exhibited by an insensitive porter. In reality, Joseph was much more in control of his own affairs than is depicted in these accounts.

He was born in Leicester in 1862 and began to experience skin and bone changes whilst still a young child. After the early death of his mother, Mary Jane Merrick (nee Potterton), his father Joseph Rockley Merrick, a factory engine driver, married again. Joseph's sister was also disabled and he was obliged to try to earn a living, first as a cigar maker and, when his right hand became too deformed to allow him to do this, by hawking trinkets through the streets. This became impossible when he was repeatedly mobbed by children. After living for a time with his uncle, Charles Barnabas Merrick, Joseph entered the Leicester Workhouse in 1879 and spent two miserable periods there over the next few years.

Eventually Joseph had the idea of trying to make some money from his misfortunes and he approached the showmen, Sam Torr and Tom Norman (known as "*The Silver King*") with a plan to exhibit himself in a travelling freak show. Norman ran the show and was comparatively kind to Joseph, in contrast to the depiction of the cruel showman by Treves and in the character of the showman named '*Bytes*' in David Lynch's film. Treves' medical students, who knew he had published articles about cases of monstrous disease, alerted him when the show was temporarily located in an empty shop in the Whitechapel Road, opposite the London Hospital in 1884.

Treves examined Merrick at his rooms in the London Hospital Medical College, where he was lecturer on anatomy, and presented him to a medical audience at a meeting of the Pathological Society of London subsequently writing up the presentation in the proceedings of the society as "a case of congenital deformity".

Returning to the sideshow, Joseph was not a success, but he put by what money he could and went to the Continent with a showman named Ferrari in the hope that he would be more successful there. His hopes were not fulfilled and were cruelly dashed when Ferrari abandoned him in Belgium and stole Joseph's savings. After a nightmarish journey via Harwich to London, Joseph was mobbed at Liverpool Street Station: the police found Treves' calling card in Joseph's pocket and brought him to the London Hospital. Struck by the pathos of Merrick's plight, the Hospital Chairman, Francis Carr-Gomm wrote to *The Times* newspaper appealing for support. A Merrick Fund was established and £250 sent in by *Times* readers with an annual donation of £50 promised by a Mr. Singer if Joseph could be kept at the hospital, which according to contemporary accounts, was what Joseph himself desired.

Joseph was not, strictly speaking, admissible as a patient under the London Hospital's byelaws, being incurable and not acutely ill, but the hospital's management, the House Committee, made him the institution's only 'inmate', a term usually reserved for the inhabitants of workhouses and asylums. A bed-sitting room and a bathroom were converted for his use in the basement of the East Wing facing Bedstead Square. A bathroom was a necessity: Joseph had to bathe every day to prevent the growths on his skin becoming foul. Treves' medical students and junior doctors and the devoted nurse, Emma Ireland, attended to him and he received visitors. In 1887 he was introduced to the Princess of Wales, the future Queen Alexandra when she was visiting the London Hospital to open a new nurses' home and medical library.

The hospital authorities also arranged for Joseph to have holidays in the country, visits to Treves' home and to a theatre. Joseph enjoyed making and giving presents and one of these, a cardboard model of Mainz Cathedral made for the actress Madge Kendall, has survived.

Joseph was found dead lying on his bed on April 11, 1890. His death certificate and the subsequent inquest record that he died of natural causes: asphyxia occasioned by the weight of his head. He had for years slept with his head resting on his knees and experienced distress when lying down: perhaps he had fallen onto his back and was not able to right himself? Treves' reminiscence records that Joseph had always wanted to sleep 'like other people' and David Lynch's film portrays Joseph deliberately lying down for his last sleep: effectively committing suicide. This suggestion is contradicted by the evidence that he was found lying across his bed, suggesting that he was getting out of bed and fell backwards on to it when he died.

A memorial service was held in the Hospital Chapel, after which Treves and his surgical colleague, Thomas Horrocks Openshaw, dissected Joseph's body, which was unclaimed by his family and which could therefore be put to educational use under the terms of the Anatomy Act. Whilst Joseph's soft tissue remains were buried, his skeleton was preserved as a specimen in the medical school museum collection. It has survived together with plaster death casts depicting his head and upper body, his arms and his right foot. Frederick Treves retired as Surgeon to the London Hospital in 1896, but continued to be an honorary consultant and an active supporter of the hospital for the rest of his life. In 1996 a new surgical ward at the London Hospital, which was granted a Royal title in 1990, was named Treves Ward in his memory.

APPENDIX I

Family Census Records

MERRICK GENEALOGY

1841
Address: Nelson Square, St. Margaret's Parish, Leicester

Residents	Age	Year	Occupation
Barnabas Merrick, head	50	1792	Wood Turner
Sarah Merrick, wife	35	1816	
Joseph Rockley Merrick	*3*	*1838*	
Henry Merrick	8m	1841	

1851
Address: 26 Lower Charles Street, St. Margaret's Parish, Leicester

Residents	Age	Year	Occupation
Barnabas Merrick, head	59	1792	Wood Turner
Sarah Merrick, wife	48	1816	
Joseph Rockley Merrick	*13*	*1838*	*Errand Boy*
Henry Merrick	10	1841	Scholar
Charles Barnabas Merrick	5	1846	

1861
Address: 20 Lee Street, St. Margaret's Parish Leicester

Residents	Age	Year	Occupation
Sarah Merrick, head, widow	45	1816	Wood Stitcher
Joseph Rockley Merrick	*23*	*1838*	*Warehouseman*

29th December 1861 - Joseph Rockley Merrick married Mary Jane Potterton at Thurmaston Parish Church, Leicester.
Marriage ref: Barrow Dec 1861 7a 353

Eldest son: JOSEPH CAREY MERRICK, born August 5th 1862. A SECOND SON, John Thomas, was born on April 21st, 1864. He lived only 3 months and died on 24th July, 1864

1865 - moved to 119 Upper Brunswick Street, Leicester
1868 - moved to 161 Birstall Street, Russel Square, Leicester

A THIRD son, William Arthur, was born in 1866. He died of Scarlet Fever.

1871
Address: 161 Birstall Street, St. Margaret's Parish, Leicester

Residents	Age	Year	Occupation
Joseph Rockley Merrick, head	33	1838	Stoker
Mary Jane Merrick, wife	33	1838	
JOSEPH CAREY MERRICK	8	1862	Scholar
Marian Eliza Merrick	3	1868	

Mary Jane Merrick died of bronchopneumonia, aged 36 on 19th May 1873.

In 1874 The family moved to 4 Wanlip Street and rented rooms from a widow, Emma Wood-Antill (nee Warner) and her two daughters. Florence and Annie (daughters of John Wood-Antill).

3rd December 1874 Joseph Rockley Merrick married Emma Wood-Antill (nee Warner) at Archdeacon Lane Baptist Church Leicester. Marriage Ref: Leicester Dec 1874 7a 600.

1875 The Merrick family moved to 37 Russell Square.
Joseph Carey Merrick left home to live with his Uncle Charles and Aunt Jane for two years, finally entering the Leicester Union Workhouse on December 26, 1879.

1881
Address: 30 Roughton St, Belgrave, St. Margaret's Parish, Leicester

Residents	Age	Year	Occupation
Joseph Rockley Merrick, head	43	1838	Stoker Dye Works
Emma Merrick, wife	37	1844	
Annie Antill	16	1865	Laundress
Florence Antill	7	1874	Scholar
Marian Eliza Merrick	13	1868	
Cassandra Merrick	2	1879	
Dora R. Merrick	0	1881	

JOSEPH CAREY MERRICK died in London (at the London Hospital) on 11th April 1890. Marion Eliza Merrick died alone on 19th March 1891, in Leicester. The cause of her death: myelitic convulsions.

1891

Address: 28 Justice Street, Belgrave, St. Margaret's Parish, Leicester

Residents	Age	Year	Occupation
Joseph Rockley Merrick, head	53	1838	Stationary Engine Driver
Emma Merrick, wife	47	1844	
Florence Wood Antill	17		Shoe Fitter/Machinist
Cassandra Merrick	12	1879	Scholar
Dora Rockley Merrick	10	1881	Scholar
Pauline Merrick	8	1883	Scholar

Emma Warner Wood Antill Merrick married George Preston in 1898. She died on 24th November, 1923.

POTTERTON GENEALOGY

1841

Address: Stoughton, Thurnby, Leicestershire

Residents	Age	Year	Occupation
William Potterton, head	40	1799	Agricultural labourer
Elizabeth Potterton, wife	30	1811	
Ann Potterton	7	1834	
Mary Jane Potterton	*4*	*1837*	
Elizabeth Potterton	3	1838	
Thomas Potterton	4	1841	

1851

Address: 9, Thurmaston, South Leicestershire

Residents	Age	Year	Occupation
William Potterton, head	49	1799	Agricultural labourer
Elizabeth Potterton, wife	44	1807	
Mary Jane Potterton	*14*	*1837*	*Servant*
Elizabeth Potterton	12	1839	Scholar
Thomas Potterton	10	1841	Scholar
Eliza Potterton	7	1844	Scholar
George Potterton	5	1846	
John Potterton	8m		

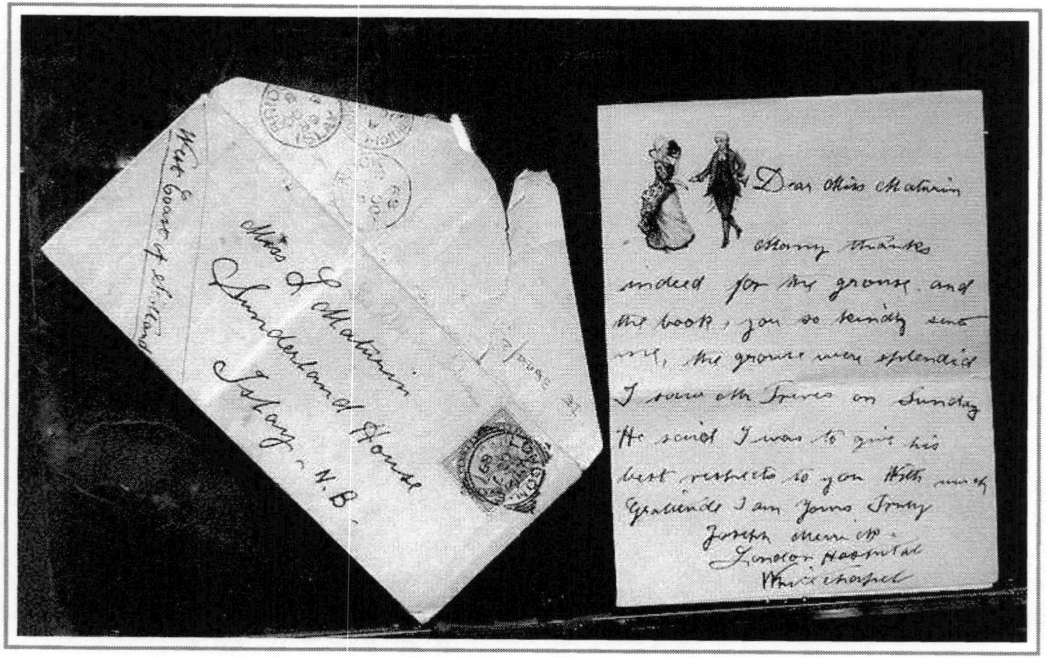

Joseph's only surviving letter, a thank-you note to Mrs. Leila Maturin. According to Treves, she was the first woman to shake his hand and smile at him.

"Dear Miss (sic) Maturin Many thanks for the books and the grouse you so kindly sent me. The grouse were splendid. I saw Mr. Treves on Sunday. He said I was to give his best respects to you. With much gratitude I am Yours Truly, Joseph Merrick
London Hospital
Whitechapel
(The Royal London Hospital Archives & Museum)

BIBLIOGRAPHY

Anonymous article," The Illustrated London Chronicle," Dec 29, 1930. British Medical Journal, Dec. 1886

Carr-Gomm, F.C. "Letter to the London Times," Dec 1886, January, 1886

Friends of Welford Cemetery Burial Records, 2011

Halsted, D.G. "A Doctor in the Nineties"

Howell, Michael & Ford, Peter. "The True History of the Elephant Man," Alison Busby, 2001

Howell, Michael & Ford, Peter. Unpublished interview with William Dooley, 2001

Kendal, Madge "Dame Madge Kendal By Herself," 1930

Leicester Mercury Newspaper, 2002-2011

Montagu, Ashley, "The Elephant Man: A Study in Human Dignity"

Norman, Thomas "Memoirs, "Howell & Ford, "The True History of the Elephant Man, Alison Busby 2001 .

Pathological Society of London, December 1886

Treves, Frederick, "The Elephant Man and Other Reminiscences," Casell, 1923 ed.

Tuckett, Reginald, Howell & Ford, "The True History of the Elephant Man, Alison Busby 2001 ed.

ON-LINE SOURCES

Access My Library
http://www.accessmylibrary.com

Beal, Susan, Proteus Syndrome Foundation USA "Glossary of Proteus Terms" http://www.proteus-syndrome.org/
Biesecker, Leslie, M.D. "Cause of Proteus Discovered, "July 2011,

National Institute of Health, National Human Genome Research
Institute, Lab for Genetic Research
http://www.genome.gov/proteus/
Birrie, H. Balcha, Jemaneh, L, Ethiop Med. Journal
http://en.wikipedia.org/wiki/Elephantiasis

Evans, Jonathan, The Joseph Carey Merrick Tribute Website, 2011
http://www.josephcareymerrick.com

Merrick, Joseph Carey "The Autobiography of Joseph Carey
Merrick," Jeanette Sitton, "Joseph Carey Merrick Tribute Website"
http://www.josephcareymerrick.com

National Human Genome Research Institute "What is Proteus
Syndrome?"
http://www.genome.gov/proteus/

Pereira, Jonathan, "The Elements of Materia Medica and
Therapeutica,
http://www.archive.org/details/elementsmateria02peregoog

Politics and Society, "The Journals of Lady Louisa Knightley,"
http://ebookee.org/Politics-and-Society-The-Journals-of-Lady-Knightley-of-Fawsley-1885-to-1913_604469.html

Sitton, Jeanette, "Joseph Carey Merrick Tribute Website"
http://www.josephcareymerrick.com

Whitewood-Neal, Tracey, Proteus Syndrome Foundation UK, 2011
http://www.proteus-syndrome.org.uk/

Windfall Films, Discovery Networks, "Meet the Elephant Man,"
first aired 29 March, 2011
http://www.discoveryuk.com/web/meet-the-elephant-man/videos/

Additional on-line sources:

"The elephant man"
Source J Audiov Media Med 1991 Apr; 14(2):59-61.

"The Plight of the Elephant Man
http://health.discovery.com/convergence/elephantman/
elephantman.html

MLA Citation for School Reports, Links, and Presentations: DR. "The Elephant Man." Doctor Secrets!
2/13/2012. http://www.doctorsecrets.com/amazing-medical-facts/elephant-man/the-elephant-man.html

"The Elephant Man's Bones Reveal Mystery"
He stumped physicians for 100 years
From Mary Kugler, R.N., former About.com Guide

"Joseph Merrick"
From Wikipedia, the free encyclopaedia

"Elephant Man Mystery Unravelled"
2006 report from BBC News

Joseph Merrick (The Elephant Man)
(5 Aug 1862 - 11 Apr 1890)

English patient. Obituary for Joseph Merrick, the "Elephant Man."
From Notes and Items in the Medical Mirror (1890)

"Meet Joseph Merrick"
http://www.discoveryuk.com/web/meet-the-elephant-man/photos/meet-joseph-merrick/

"The Elephant Man's Mistaken Identity"
by D. Trull, Enigma Editor
dtrull@parascope.com

"The Store of an Outcast: Joseph Merrick (The Elephant Man)
(5 Aug 1862 - 11 Apr 1890)
From The Speaker (London, 1890)

GLOSSARY OF PROTEUS TERMS

Terms and definitions often associated with Proteus Syndrome. Compiled by Susan Beachler

A

ADIPOSE – pertaining to fat
ALVEOLAR RIDGES- the part of the jaw containing the tooth sockets
ANAEROBIC- able to live without oxygen
ANISOCORIA – unequal pupil size
ANKYLOSIS – stiff joint
ANOMALY- not normal
ANTERIOR – before; in front of
ASYMMETRY- both sides not alike; not symmetrical

B

BILATERAL – relating to two sides
BRAIN MALFORMATIONS – failure of proper brain development

C

CAFE-AU-LAIT – pale brown areas on the skin
CARIOUS – tooth decay
CAVERNOUS – hollow
CHALONES – a substance that regulates cell division
CHOROID – dark brown vascular coat of the eye
CHOROIRETINITIS – inflammation of the choroid and retina
CHROMOSOME – contains DNA- a linear thread in the nucleus of a cell- usually normal in PROTEUS
CLINICAL – founded on actual observation or treatment
CLINODACTYLY – permanent deflection of one or more fingers

CONSANGUINITY – relationship by blood
CRANIAL HEMIHYPERTROPHY- increased muscular bulk on one side of the skull
CRANIOSYNOSTIS – premature closure of skull bones
CRANIUM – skull
CREATINE KINASE – enzyme present in skeletal and cardiac muscle and the brain
CUTANEOUS – skin

D

DANDY-WALKER CYST — congenital hydrocephalus caused by a blockage in the brain
DELINEATED — outlined
DENTITION — the type, number, and arrangement of teeth
DEPIGMENTATION — loss of pigment; partial or complete
DOLICHOCEPHALY — a long front to the back diameter of the skull
DYSMORPHIC — not in normal form
DYSPNEA — laboured breathing
DYSTROPHIC — not in the right place

E

EPIBULBAR – located on the eyeball
EPIPHYSEOLYSIS – disease of the bone-making centre of long bones or pineal gland
EPITHELIUM – skin (epidermis & mucous membranes)
ESOTROPIA – crossed eyes
EXOSTOSIS – a bony growth that grows on a bone

F

FEMUR – thigh bone
FLEXION CONTRACTURE – a bent joint that doesn't extend

H

HALLUX – the great toe
HAMARTOMA – a benign tumour
HAMARTONEOPLASTIC – a building of benign tumours
HEMANGIOMA – a benign tumour of the large blood vessels
HEMIHYPERTROPHY – half of the body size increased
HEMIMEGALENCEPHALY – half of the brain is larger
HETEROCHROMIA IRIDES – different eye colours
HIRSUTISM – excessive growth of hair in unusual places
HYPERKERATOSIS – overgrowth of skin or tumours made of keratin (tough protein found in hair and nails)
HYPERKERATOTIC LESION – overgrowth of cornea
HYPEROSTOSIS – overgrowth of bone
HYPERPIGMENTED – extra colour in the skin
HYPERTROPHY – increased size of an organ or the body

I

INFERIOR – below

K

KYPHOSIS – humpback
KYPHOSCOLIOSIS – curvature of the spine with humpback

L

LINEAR – a line
LIPOMA – a fatty tumour
LORDOSCOLIOSIS – forward curve of the spine with lateral curve
LUMBOSACRAL – lower back
LYPHANGIOMA – tumour consisting of lymphatic tissue

M

MACROCEPHALY – abnormally large head
MACRODACTYLY – abnormally large fingers and toes
MACRO-ORCHIDISM – abnormally large testicles
MACULE – flat discoloured spot on the skin
MEGALOPODIA – abnormally large feet
MERRICK, JOSEPH – 1862-1890, "Elephant Man" probably had Proteus syndrome
METATARSALS – bones just behind the toes
MICROPHTHALMIA – abnormally small eyes
MONOMORPHIC ADENOMA – unchangeable tumour
MORBIDITY – diseased

N

NEOPLASM – tumour or growth
NEOPLASTIC – the nature of abnormal tissue
NEVI – (plural of nevus) a mole or birthmark
NYSTAGMUS – constant, involuntary, cyclical movement of the eyeball

O

ORCHIDOPEXY – surgery to transfer undescended testicles to the scrotum
OSSIFICATION – process of making bone

P

PACHYDERMATOCELES – a hanging tumour
PALATE – roof of the mouth
PALLOR – lack of colour
PAPILLOMA – benign tumour without blood vessels
PATELLAE – knee cap

PATHOGENIC – productive of disease
PHALANGES – bones in fingers and toes
PLANTAR HYPERPLASIA – extra thick skin on the soles of feet
POLMORPHOUS – occurring in more than one form
PORT OF WINE STAIN – purple-red birthmark
POSTERIOR – toward the back
PROTEUS – a Greek god- a polymorphous who could change his shape at will to escape capture
PTOSIS – drooping of an organ

R

RADIOGRAPH – x-ray
RETINAL COLOBOMAS – a lesion on the retina
RETROPERITONEAL – where kidneys are located, outside the peritoneal cavity behind the peritoneum

M

MACROCEPHALY – abnormally large head
MACRODACTYLY – abnormally large fingers and toes
MACRO-ORCHIDISM – abnormally large testicles
MACULE – flat discoloured spot on the skin
MEGALOPODIA – abnormally large feet
MERRICK, JOSEPH – 1862-1890, "Elephant Man" probably had Proteus syndrome
METATARSALS – bones just behind the toes
MICROPHTHALMIA – abnormally small eyes
MONOMORPHIC ADENOMA – unchangeable tumour
MORBIDITY – diseased

N

NEOPLASM – tumour or growth

NEOPLASTIC – the nature of abnormal tissue
NEVI – (plural of nevus) a mole or birthmark
NYSTAGMUS – constant, involuntary, cyclical movement of the eyeball

O

ORCHIDOPEXY – surgery to transfer undescended testicles to the scrotum
OSSIFICATION – process of making bone

P

PACHYDERMATOCELES – a hanging tumour
PALATE – roof of the mouth
PALLOR – lack of colour
PAPILLOMA – benign tumour without blood vessels
PATELLAE – knee cap
PATHOGENIC – productive of disease
PHALANGES – bones in fingers and toes
PLANTAR HYPERPLASIA – extra thick skin on the soles of feet
POLMORPHOUS – occurring in more than one form
PORT OF WINE STAIN – purple-red birthmark
POSTERIOR – toward the back
PROTEUS – a Greek god- a polymorphous who could change his shape at will to escape capture
PTOSIS – drooping of an organ

R

RADIOGRAPH – x-ray
RETINAL COLOBOMAS – a lesion on the retina
RETROPERITONEAL – where kidneys are located, outside the peritoneal cavity behind the peritoneum

S

SCOLIOSIS – curvature of the spine
SHAGREEN – leathery
STRABISMUS – straying eye
SULCIFORM – a groove, especially of the brain
SUPERIOR – higher or above
SYNDACTYLY – webbed fingers or toes

T

TALIPES – any deformity of the foot
TELANGIECTASIS – a vascular lesion of the blood vessels-looks like a birthmark
TIBIA – the large bone of the lower leg
TRAGUS – a projection made of cartilage in front of the ear canal
TRANSVERSE PROCESS – crossways bone or tissue

V

VALGUS – bowlegged-bent outward
VARICOSITIES – distended, swollen, knotted veins
VERRUCOUS EPIDERMAL – wart like skin
VISCERAL – internal organs, especially abdominal

W

WHORLED – a spiral arrangement

Courtesy of the Proteus Syndrome Foundation
http://www.proteus-syndrome.org/
Kim Hoag, Founder

In Loving Memory of
Alexander Hoag
7/5/90 - 9/20/99
"He did a lot in 9 short years."

LIST OF ILLUSTRATIONS

The following is a description of illustrations and photographs that can be found throughout this book.

Page 7   The **Royal London Hospital,** Whitechapel, London

Page 18   **Thurmaston Parish Church**, where Mary Jane Potterton and Joseph Rockley Merrick were wed, December 29, 1861.

Page 19   **Humberstone Gate** in Leicester, where Mary Jane is said to have been knocked down by a circus elephant when pregnant with Joseph in May, 1862. Joseph believed her 'fright' was the cause of his condition.

Page 20   **Most of the original Lee Street**, where Joseph was born on August 5, 1862, has long gone. This is the only section surviving. Although at some point resurfaced, 19th century cobbles peep through. Now renamed Lower Lee Street. Joseph's home would have been just a few feet from the dip in the pavement, behind the fencing. (top left) (Jeanette Sitton, FoJCM, copyright 2012 all rights reserved).

Page 21   The Birth Certificate of Joseph Carey Merrick. Registered at two years of age.

Page 28   **Churchgate Street,** where Joseph's Uncle Charles ran a barbershop, though not shown.

Page 29   **Archdeacon Lane Baptist Church**, where Mary Jane taught Sunday School and Joseph attended church.

Page 30   Boys in **Syston Street School**, circa 1910. Joseph attended there in the 1860s.

Page 31   The newly discovered **grave of Mary Jane Potterton and William Arthur Merrick**. Also interred there are her siblings, John, Ann and Elizabeth Potterton.

Page 32   Typical wares of a **haberdashery** shop.

Page 33   The **Clock Tower in Haymarket Square** where Joseph often hawked wares from his father's haberdashery.

Page 34   A typical 19th century square in Leicester's poorer quarter.

Page 41   The **workhouse entry for December 29th, 1979**, showing Joseph's first workhouse entry (second line). His occupation is listed as "hawker," the church is left blank, and he gives his birth year as 1861.

Page 42   **Leicester Union Workhouse**, where Joseph lived and worked from 1879 to 1883.

Page 43   Inmates of the **Whitechapel Workhouse**, a short distance from Spitalfields.

Page 44   The **family grave of the Merrick family**. The resting place of Marion Eliza Merrick, Joseph Rockley Merrick, and Emma Wood-Antill Merrick. Belgrave Cemetery, Leicester.

Page 60   **Layout of the London Hospital**, 1886

213

Page 61	**The disguise Joseph Merrick wore**, to hide his deformity.
Page 62	**Tom Norman**, Joseph's London Manager. His Whitechapel exhibition was across the road from the London Hospital, where several doctors came to see him, including Frederick Treves.
Page 63	**Tom Norman's sideshow**.
Page 64	**Joseph Merrick in 1884**, before his presentation before the London Hospital Pathological Society (believed to be a sketch by Frederick Treves).
Page 65	**Liverpool Street Station**, where Joseph arrived after a disastrous tour of the Continent in June, 1886. Robbed and starving, he arrived here and was mobbed by a crowd, as poignantly reenacted in the 1980 film, "The Elephant Man." (public domain).
Page 66	**A view of 19th century Whitechapel** and the London Hospital. The new Grocer's hospital wing stands to the left of the clock.
Page 67	**The Royal London Hospital**. Rare photos taken by Jeanette Sitton. The closest one can get to the original Isolation Ward, where Frederick Treves sheltered Joseph. The hospital's facade clock is just off the corridor.
Page 74	**Francis Culling Carr-Gomm**, Hospital Governor who lobbied on Joseph's behalf for permanent housing at the London Hospital.
Page 74	**Sir Frederick Treves**, Joseph's friend and doctor.

Page 75   **Princess Alexandra** visits the London Hospital on May 23, 1878. After opening the new Alexandra Wing and visiting the general wards, she and the Prince of Wales paid a special visit to Joseph.

Page 76   The door and window of **Joseph's rooms in Bedstead Square** and the original steps that led down, from Bedstead Square. The entrance to Joseph's rooms in Bedstead Square.

Page 77   The **hospital gardens** where Joseph took walks at night, being unable to come out by daylight.

Page 78   **Joseph's armchair**, specially designed for him by William Taylor, the hospital engineer who also outfitted his rooms with a bath and bed-sitting room. *(Courtesy of the Taylor family)*.

Page 78   The distinguished actress, **Dame Madge Kendal**, Joseph's friend and patron. She sent him many gifts and sponsored his known trip to Drury Lane Theatre. However, they probably never met in person, though he hoped she would come to receive the model church he constructed for her.

Page 79   The **card Cathedral that Joseph built**. It was made from a kit, and is of Mainz Cathedral, Germany.

Page 80   Mainz Cathedral kit. The exact same model that Joseph built. It was published before 1893 by Joseph Scholz, as part of the series 'Little Master Builder'. (Reverend Thomas Clay. Copyright 2012. All rights reserved)

Page 85   **A gentleman's vanity case** which probably looks similar to the one Joseph used.

215

Page 96   **Handing over of the plaque to the Moat Community College**, Leicester.

Page 101   **Fawsley Hall Estate**, the private estate of Lady Louisa Knightley, who sponsored three holidays for Joseph on her estate. The Manor is now a hotel.

Page 102   **Lady Louisa Knightley** (1842–1913).

Page 102   **Red Hill Farm**, where Joseph stayed in the Autumn of 1889.

Page 103   **St. Mary the Virgin church**, inside the once Fawsley Estate.

Page 103   **Alabaster tomb of Sir Richard Knightley and his wife Jane Skenard**, heiress to Old Aldington. c1540.

Page 113   **Dr Leslie Biesecker**, Researcher, National Institute of Health Human Genome Project.

Page 115   **Mosaicism in Proteus Syndrome**, National Institute of Health Human Genome Project.

Page 120   **Inquest into the death of Joseph Merrick.** (Friends of Joseph Carey Merrick website).

Page 121   **A computerised, scientific recreation of Joseph's face** had he not developed Proteus Syndrome and possible NF1, based on scans of his relatives on both the Potterton and Merrick sides. (Discovery Health, "The Plight of the Elephant Man, 2002).

Page 125   **Jordan Whitewood-Neal** (2011).

Page 129 **Lisa Bartlett.**

Page 131 **Brian Richards.**

Page 143 **Reverend Thomas Clay.**

Page 145-6 Views of an extremely rare, modern version, of the **Mainz Cathedral kit.**

Page 147 **Joseph Merrick poses in his Sunday Best suit** for a visiting card, (carte de visite), circa 1889. He gave one of these to his spiritual counsellor, Reverend Tristram Valentine, and then passed on to a doctor's family before being returned to the London Hospital. It is the only known photograph of Joseph seated and fully dressed. (Royal London Hospital Museum Archives).

Page 190 **Joseph Merrick in 1889.**

Page 200 **Joseph's only surviving letter,** a thank-you note to Mrs. Leila Maturin written in 1889.. According to Treves, she was the first woman to shake his hand and smile at him. (Leicester Register's Office).

Page 227 **The Hippodrome, (Gaiety) Theatre building,** Leicester.

APPENDICES

APPENDIX A - page 113
What is Proteus Syndrome?
An article by Dr. Leslie Biesecker
Frequently Asked Questions

APPENDIX B - page 122
Being the mother of a Proteus child:
An essay by Tracey Whitewood-Neal, MBE
of the Proteus Syndrome Foundation UK

APPENDIX C - page 125
Jordan Whitewood-Neal's story
Lisa Bartlett's story
Brian Richards' story

APPENDIX D - page 143
Building Joseph's cathedral

APPENDIX E - page 149
The "Elephant Man and Other Reminiscences",
by Frederick Treves

APPENDIX F - page 173
"The Penny Showman", Tom Norman's Memoirs

APPENDIX G - page 184
"Frederick Treves vs Tom Norman: Another perspective"
by Gerry LeFurgy, Historian, FoJCM

APPENDIX H - page 191
"Joseph Carey Merrick: Patient by Another Name",
by Jonathan Evans, Archivist, the Royal London Hospital Archive
and Museum

APPENDIX I - page 197
Family Census records

INDEX

Alexandra, Queen, King Edward (Princess Alexandra, Prince of Wales) 71, 72, 75, 82, 98, 109, 163, 164, 191, 195, 215, 219
Amputation 123, 132
Andrews, Glen 95
Anglican 92
Animal 10, 27, 48, 104, 119, 149, 169, 175, 182
Anonymous 9, 112, 201
Antill, Emma Wood 13, 44, 97, 198, 199, 213
Archdeacon Lane Baptist Church 12, 13, 29, 97, 198, 212
Armchair, Joseph's 78, 215, 219
Asphyxiation 92, 93, 99
Asylum 160, 187, 195
Autobiography, of Joseph Merrick 5, 10, 16, 17, 22, 26, 35, 36, 40, 70, 84, 104, 191, 202
Barnum, P.T. 37
Bartlett, Lisa 3, 125, 129, 130, 216, 218
Bedstead Square 60, 68, 69, 72, 76, 77, 91, 156, 160, 161, 163, 170, 187, 195, 215
Beehive Inn 106
Beggar 39, 183
Belgium 36, 52, 86, 98, 154, 194
Beloved 55, 82, 166
Bible 9, 56, 91, 157
Biesecker, Dr. Leslie 3, 113, 116, 218
Bodyguard 61, 90, 187
Books 12, 48, 56, 70, 71, 81, 87, 90, 109, 157, 160, 163, 171, 200
British Library 3, 40, 49
British Medical Journal 5, 49, 56, 107, 110, 112, 201
Bronchial pneumonia 13, 97, 198
Brussels 98, 154
Bully 12, 135, 139
Bunsen burner 150, 180, 181
Burdett Couttes, Baroness 82
Butt, Stephen 3, 31, 95, 96
Cardew, Wardell 52
Carr-Gomm, Francis Culling 5, 51, 57, 58, 59, 70, 71, 73, 74, 86, 98, 99, 111, 112, 156, 194, 201, 214
Carte de Visite 217, 219
Cathedral, card 3, 68, 79, 80, 143, 144, 195, 215, 217, 218

Charity 23, 39, 58, 91, 176, 182
Childhood 5, 86, 108, 127, 158
Christmas 5, 23, 24, 72, 81, 140, 164, 165
Churchgate Street 22, 28, 97, 212
Cigar Factory 14, 97, 186
Clay, Reverend Thomas 3, 68, 80, 143, 145, 146, 217
Clock Tower 14, 15, 33
Cohen, Michael Jr. DMD, Ph.D 114
Comfort 10, 12, 14, 104, 111, 165, 174, 177, 180
Comfortable 22, 25, 36, 39, 54, 59, 70, 89, 106, 109, 133, 156, 158,
Commemorative plaque - 5, 96
Commissioners for Hackney Carriages 23
Compassionate 70, 181
Continent 51, 57, 65, 154, 183, 193,194, 214
Costume 27, 153
Cousins, Peter 3, 44
Couttes, Burdett, Baroness 219
Curtain 38, 46, 150, 153, 162, 165, 169, 175-178, 180
Dale, Rob 3, 17
Death 8, 11, 13, 22, 35, 69, 91, 92, 93, 99, 104, 118, 120, 133, 135, 171, 191-193, 195, 198, 216
Death Certificate 11, 195
Deformity 10, 14, 27, 55, 57, 61, 104, 105, 107, 108, 112, 161, 165, 166, 187, 194, 210, 214
Dignity 8, 26, 36, 39, 83, 95, 174, 201
Discomfort 133
Disguise 36, 47, 51, 53, 61, 152
DNA 114, 118, 204
Dooley, Bertram 51, 90 187
Dooley, William 51, 54, 201
Dorchester, 100, 109
Dressing case (vanity case) 81
Drew, Rose 93
Drury Lane Theatre 26, 26, 78, 81, 82, 84, 95, 99, 167, 168, 169, 195, 215, 217, 219
Edward, King Queen Alexandra (Wales, Prince and Princess Alexandra) 71, 72, 75, 82, 98, 109, 163, 164, 191, 195, 215, 219
Elephant 104, 107, 149, 175, 176, 193, 214
Elephant Man 1, 5, 8, 9, 10, 11, 17, 19, 26, 27, 36, 37, 38, 40, 45, 46, 47, 48, 51, 54, 56, 57, 59, 65, 72, 73, 84, 87, 89, 94, 98, 100, 104, 106, 107, 108, 109, 110, 111, 113, 114, 121, 122, 131, 142, 149, 150, 151, 152, 154, 156, 160, 161, 165,

166, 167, 173, 174, 175, 176, 177, 182, 183, 184, 185, 186, 187, 189, 191, 192, 201
Elephant Man, the True History of the 11, 17, 26, 40, 49, 54, 59, 73, 84, 89, 94, 106, 110, 189, 201
Ellis, Mr. 35, 47, 106, 185
Epstein, Ruth 93
Escape 14, 26, 89, 152, 161, 171, 208, 209
Evans, Jonathan 3, 73, 94, 191, 218
Examination 69, 116, 153, 179, 188
Exhaustion 156
Exhibition 35, 36, 45, 50, 62, 113, 149, 153, 154, 159
Fair 6, 10, 35, 47, 50, 57, 90, 158, 159, 171, 173, 174
Fairground 8, 35, 46
False Greatness 2, 36, 70
Farm, Red Hill 89, 102
Fawsley Estate 3, 99, 101, 102, 103, 216
Feelings 55, 89, 126, 135, 157, 166, 167
Fordington Cemetery 100, 109
Freak 15, 27, 35, 50, 98, 149, 182, 194
Freeman's Cigar Factory, Messrs. 14, 105
Friends of Joseph Carey Merrick (FoJCM) 1-4, 6, 18, 20, 31, 67, 75-78, 95, 96, 100, 184, 212, 216
Friends of Welford Road Cemetery 3
Gaiety Theatre 26, 27, 36, 40, 95, 229
Gamekeeper 89, 170
Genetic Disease 119
Genetic Disease Research Branch 113, 119
Gladstone Vaults 26, 27, 40, 105, 229
Grenfell, Wilfred 87
Grouse 90, 200
Hackney Carriages, Commissioners for 23
Hartley, Emma-Jane 3, 102
Harwich 52, 194
Hawking 14-16, 22, 23, 33, 35, 41, 105, 185, 186, 193, 213
Haymarket Square 14, 33
Heroic 84, 165, 171
Hippodrome 26, 229
Hitchcock, George 35-37, 173
Horror 15, 25, 39, 46, 55, 57, 87, 153, 158, 167, 176
Howell & Ford 11, 17, 26, 40, 49, 54, 59, 73, 84, 94, 106, 189
Humberstone Gate 10, 19, 212, 221

Illustrated London Chronicle 201
Incurable 53, 57, 59, 156, 195
Indecency 48, 51, 52
Institution 58, 109 195
Ireland, Nurse Emma 53, 57, 69, 92, 183, 192
Isaac Watts 2, 36, 70
Isolation 53, 55, 57, 67, 83, 92, 156, 214
Joseph Carey Merrick Tribute website 4, 110, 202
Journey 52, 86, 122, 154, 156, 159, 171, 194
Kantrowitz, Audrey 2, 67, 79, 95, 184
Kavia, Cllr. Ramnik (Lord Mayor of Leicester) 95
Kendall, William and Madge 52, 68, 72, 78, 82, 87, 89, 195, 201
Kindness 6, 36, 58, 67, 70, 87, 90, 95, 96, 106, 111, 118, 126, 136, 152, 155, 156, 158, 159, 161, 162, 163, 164, 165, 168, 169, 170, 174, 177, 184, 194, 200
King Edward, Queen Alexandra (Wales, Prince and Princess Alexandra) 71, 72, 75, 82, 98, 109, 163, 164, 191, 195, 215, 219
Knightley, Lady Louisa 72, 84, 88, 89, 101, 102, 103, 169, 202, 216
Lee Street 9, 12, 20, 27, 104, 197, 212,
LeFurgy, Gerry 39, 49, 184, 218
Legs, Joseph Merrick's 47, 104, 118, 122, 123, 126, 171
Leicester 3, 9, 12-15, 17, 19, 20, 23, 25, 26, 27, 29, 30, 31, 33, 34, 36, 41, 42, 44, 50, 52, 57, 86, 91, 95, 96, 97-99, 104, 105, 107, 112, 173, 176, 186, 189, 192-194, 197-199, 201, 212, 213, 215, 217, 219
Leicester Mercury 3, 15, 28, 29, 30, 33, 34, 41, 42, 62, 96, 201, 219
Leicester Union Workhouse 5, 15, 22-27, 38, 41-43, 51, 52, 57, 58, 87, 95, 98, 160, 167, 174, 176, 177, 186, 194, 195, 198, 213
Letter(s) 2, 5, 37, 51, 54, 57, 58, 59, 72, 73, 90, 92, 94, 98, 99, 111, 114, 118, 156, 164, 170, 174, 200, 201, 217
Lighthouse 55, 87, 160, 161
Little George 36, 173, 174
Liverpool Street train station 53, 65, 88, 98, 154, 155, 158, 194, 214
London Hospital (Royal) 8, 27, 39, 43, 45-47, 51, 53, 56-57, 59-60, 62, 66, 67, 69, 70, 74, 75, 76, 77, 79, 81, 86, 90, 97-99, 109, 112, 114, 120, 147, 148, 149, 155, 174, 183, 187, 190, 191, 194-196, 198, 200, 214-215, 217
London Times, 51, 54, 57, 59, 73, 98, 99, 120, 201
Lord Mayor, Leicester (Cllr. Ramnik Kavia) 95
Lynch, David 191, 192, 194, 195
Maturin, Leila 56, 71, 90, 91, 94, 200, 217
Medical College, London Hospital 60, 72, 99, 152, 194
Merrick, Charles Barnabas 16, 22, 23, 28, 35, 97, 194, 197, 198, 212
Merrick, John Thomas 10, 11, 13, 97, 197

Merrick, Joseph Carey:

Show name origins of, 8
Internet pages of, 8
Personal character of, 6, 9, 36, 38, 39, 48, 58, 70, 87, 183, 184-188
Physical appearance of, 8-10, 14, 23, 36-38, 48, 50, 57, 59, 71, 104-108, 113, 151-152, 173
Possible causes of the condition, 10, 38, 47, 48, 104, 113-116
Birth, 9
Christening, 9
Parents, marriage of, 9
Infancy and early years, 9-11
Onset of symptoms, 9-10
Younger brother's discovery, 10
Other siblings, 9-10
Mother's failing health and death, 13
Father's remarriage and mistreatment of, 14
Stepmother's abuse of, 14-16
Uncle Charles and Aunt Jane's care of, 16, 22-23
Workhouse years, 22-26
Surgery for removal of tumour, 26
Becomes the *Elephant Man*, 37-49
Exhibits with showmen, 27-39, 50-52, 152, 153, 157, 158, 173-180
Robbed and return to London, 52, 154
Sheltered by Frederick Treves, 53-59, 155-157
Sexuality, 55, 56, 166-168
Receives gifts from Madge Kendall, 152-163
Builds cardboard cathedral and other models, 68, 79, 144
Life in Bedstead Square, 68-70
Meets HRH Princess Alexandra, 71, 72, 163
Christmas pantomime and evening at the theatre, 81-83, 167, 168
Holidays in the countryside, 86-89, 169, 170
Decline in health, 90, 91
Death and autopsy, 92-94
Commemoration of, 95, 96

Merrick, Joseph Rockley 9, 11, 12-14, 16, 18, 35, 44, 97, 99, 193, 198, 197-199, 212, 213
Merrick, Marion Eliza 12, 44, 97, 99, 198, 213
Merrick, William Arthur 12, 13, 31, 97, 197, 213
Messrs. Freeman's Cigar Factory 14, 105

Mile End (shop) 89, 149, 154 170
Moat Community College 3, 23, 95, 96
Money 46, 65, 111, 156, 165, 183, 188, 194
Moreno, Benjamin 93
Mother 9, 10, 13, 16, 27, 35, 38, 46, 58, 91, 92, 97, 104, 108, 122, 126, 139, 158, 161, 167, 179, 193, 218
National Human Genome Research Institute 116, 202
National Institute of Health Human Genome Project 3, 115
Neurofibromatosis 121
Norman, Tom 35-40, 45, 46, 48-50, 52, 54, 57, 62, 63, 71, 73, 87, 94, 173, 178, 179, 184, 185, 187-189, 194, 201, 214
NF1 (Neurofibromatosis 1) 121, 216
Northampton(shire) 88, 99
Oakum picking 24
Old Receiving Room 192
Openshaw, Thomas Horrocks 94, 99, 196
Osseous 108, 151
Ostend 52
Pamphlet 10, 13, 35, 36, 39, 50, 70, 176, 182, 193
Pantomime 82, 167, 168
Papilloma, (papillomatous) 107, 108, 207, 209
Penny Showman 37, 40, 49, 54, 73, 173
Photograph 2, 8, 47, 50, 56, 57, 63, 71, 72, 148, 164, 212, 217
Photographer 4
Pneumonia, bronchial 13, 97, 198
Police 48, 50, 51, 52, 53, 83, 152-156, 169, 178, 194
Potterton, Mary Jane 3, 9, 10-13, 18, 19, 29, 20, 31, 58, 97, 193, 197-199, 212, 213
Proteus Syndrome (PS) 3, 4, 113-114, 115, 116-119, 121-124, 125, 126-127, 129-130, 131, 132-136, 138, 140, 142, 201-202, 204, 207-208, 210, 216, 218,
PS children 123
Puss In Boots 82, 84
Queen Alexandra, King Edward (Wales, Prince and Princess Alexandra) 71, 72, 75, 82, 98, 109, 163, 164, 191, 195, 215, 219
Record Office, for Leicestershire, Leicester and Rutland 3
Red Hill Farm 89, 102
Richards, Brian 3, 125, 131, 142, 126, 218
Roper, Sam 35, 47, 50, 51, 90
Royal London Hospital 3, 7, 45, 61, 64, 67-69, 73, 74, 77, 79, 88-89, 114, 120, 147, 148, 190, 191-192, 200, 212, 214, 217-218,
Rubin, John 93

Rutland County Registrar's Office 3
Scovil, Brooke 2
Sergeant Surgeon 109
Sideshow 10, 13, 35, 51, 63, 98, 186, 194, 214
Sitton, Jeanette 1, 2, 4, 6, 18, 20, 31, 40, 67, 75-76, 78, 95-96, 184, 202, 212, 214, 219
Sleep 55, 71, 92, 93, 123, 133, 156, 171, 195
Smart, Lynda 3
Speech 14, 23, 25, 51, 71, 72, 82, 87, 91, 93, 126, 153, 155, 157, 163, 168, 187
Spitalfields 43, 45, 52, 213
St. Michael and All Angels Church 9
Steel, Walter 90
Stepmother, Joseph's 16, 29, 35, 105
Stevenson, Robert Louis 91
Stroshane, Mae Siu-Wai 1-2, 4
Stroshane, Maya 3
Sunday Best suit 147
Sunday School 9, 12, 29, 212
Surgeon 5, 8, 25, 39, 45, 56, 71, 87-89, 91-93, 98, 109-110, 123, 132-133, 189, 191, 196
Sympathetic 36, 39, 46, 156, 181
Syston Street School 12, 30, 213
Theatre, Drury Lane 26, 26, 78, 81, 82, 84, 95, 99, 167, 168, 169, 195, 215, 217, 219
Thurmaston 9, 18, 97, 197, 199, 212
Timmons, Jeffrey 3
Timmons, Rebecca 40, 77, 219
Torr, Sam 26, 27, 35, 98, 105, 186, 187, 194
Treves, Frederick, (Sir) 5, 8, 39, 40, 45, 47-51, 53-59, 62, 64, 69-74, 81, 82-84, 86-94, 97-100, 107, 109-185, 187, 188, 189, 190, 191, 192, 193, 194, 195, 196, 200, 201, 214, 217
Trunk 10, 50, 107, 151
Tuckett, Dr. Reginald 39, 45, 59, 87, 177, 178, 181, 201
Upper-class 184
Vaccaro, Alex 93, 94
Variola (Smallpox) 11, 97
Visitors 55, 71, 72, 81, 92, 162, 165, 175, 182, 195
Wales, Prince and Princess (King Edward, Queen Alexandra) 71, 72, 75, 82, 98, 109, 163, 164, 191, 195, 215, 219
Whitechapel 7, 38, 43, 45, 46, 60, 62, 66, 89, 90, 98, 109, 112, 173, 194, 200, 212, 213, 214

Whitewood-Neal, Jordan 3, 122-124, 125, 126, 128, 216
Whitewood-Neal, Tracey 122, 125, 126, 202
Wombwell's Circus 10
Workhouse, Leicester Union 5, 15, 22-27, 38, 41-43, 51, 52, 57, 58, 87, 95, 98, 160, 167, 174, 176, 177, 186, 194, 195, 198
www.proteus-syndrome.org.uk 124, 202

The Gaiety (Hippodrome) theatre building, a hall of varieties. It was here that Joseph had his first job as a curiosity. Photo taken in the 1970s. (Leicester Mercury)

The theatre was on the corner of Wharf Street South and Gladstone Street, Leicester. A century later, it was to become a car spares company (GE Motors), and later to become Hex Holdings. The building was finally demolished in around 2010.

Inside the Gaiety there were steps leading down to the original vaults, known as Gladstone Vaults, where Joseph was on show. A member of the car company staff, in 2004, invited Jeanette Sitton and Rebecca Timmons (FoJCM) to take a look. They declined.

In 2012, wildflowers and foxes have moved in. Attractive, purple Buddleia now grows on the empty site, while awaiting the construction of a high rise building.

The development company were originally planning on calling their new block, 'Elephant House'. Following public outcry, the name has been changed to 'Merrick House'.

Printed in Great Britain
by Amazon.co.uk, Ltd.,
Marston Gate.